THE WOMEN'S BUSINESS RESOURCE GUIDE

A National Directory of Over 600
Programs, Resources and Organizations
to Help Women Start or Expand a Business

Barbara Littman and Michael Ray

The Resource Group
A Division of Information Design Northwest

P.O. Box 25505
Eugene OR 97402
(503) 683-5330

THE WOMEN'S BUSINESS RESOURCE GUIDE

A National Directory of Over 600
Programs, Resources and Organizations
to Help Women Start or Expand a Business

Barbara Littman and Michael Ray

Copyright © 1994 Information Design Northwest

All rights reserved. No part of this book may be reproduced or transmitted in any form by any means without the permission of the publisher, except by a reviewer who may quote brief passages in a review.

ISBN 1-884565-01-8 (softcover)

ISSN 1072-9801 (softcover)

Printed in the United States of America

Special Sales

This book is available for bulk purchase for sales promotions and premiums at special discounts. Special editions, including personalized covers and corporate imprints, can be printed in large quantities. For more information, contact The Resource Group.

Table of Contents

ACKNOWLEDGMENTS iv

INTRODUCTION v

A GUIDE TO FEDERAL AGENCIES viii

Chapter 1: Training, Technical Assistance and Counseling 1
    Federal Resources 2
    State Government Resources 12
    Private Resources 13

Chapter 2: Information Sources 23
    Federal Resources 24
    State Resources 31
    Private Resources 36

Chapter 3: Selling to the Government 45
    Selling to the Federal Government 46
    Selling to State Governments 52
    Private Sources of Procurement Information 54

Chapter 4: Membership Organizations 57
    Women's Business Associations 58
    Women's Professional Associations 61
    General Business Associations 64

Chapter 5: Resource, Program and Agency Listings 67
    Quick-Find Guide 68

A QUICK GUIDE TO COMMON TERMS 127

ABOUT THE AUTHORS 128

INDEX 129

SUBMISSION AND CORRECTION FORM 132

ORDERING INFORMATION 133

Acknowledgments

We would like to thank the hundreds of individuals in private and government offices and organizations who graciously sent us material about their programs, answered our questions and enthusiastically encouraged us to complete this project. If there are any errors of fact, we take complete responsibility for them.

We also want to thank the following individuals who generously gave their time to review and comment on an early draft of this book: Brenda Black, Women's Business Specialist for the U.S. Department of Commerce; Louise Chamberland, Executive Director of the Maine Women's Business Development Center; Sharon Hadary, Executive Director of The National Foundation for Women Business Owners; Harriet Fredman, Senior Project Manager for the SBA's Office of Women's Business Ownership; Geraldine Larkin, author and Manager for Emerging Business Services with Deloitte & Touche. Special thanks are due Brenda Black and Harriet Fredman for their willingness to spend the extra time needed to carefully review descriptions of federal programs.

We would also like to thank Donna Freshman for initial research and data entry, Donella Ingham for proofreading and editing assistance and Roy Paul Nelson, Professor of Journalism at the University of Oregon (and author and cartoonist in his own right) for his review of our cover design.

Introduction

Why This Book

Women are going into business in record numbers. According to government sources, they are starting businesses at two to five times the rate of men, and they currently own 30 percent of all businesses in this country. By the year 2000, that number is expected to reach or surpass 50 percent.

The businesses women start often grow more slowly than do those started by men, but statistics indicate that their enterprises have a 75 percent success rate compared with a 20 percent success rate for businesses overall. And as employers of over 11 million workers in this country, women are making significant contributions to the American economy.

But women entrepreneurs face special challenges. Money and knowledge (and often respect) don't come easily. And while succeeding in business can be a tough proposition for anyone, the special challenges women face can often mean working overtime just to get to square one.

This guide is designed to level the playing field a little by helping potential and current women entrepreneurs get started faster and move on sooner to the growth and stability that ensure success.

About This Guide

This guide covers resources available across the country that can assist women in starting, stabilizing and expanding their businesses. It emphasizes special opportunities just for women, but also includes other resources that are too good to be ignored.

We focus primarily on programs that are available nationally, directing you to offices or people in your local area whenever possible. The sections on state resources are an exception to this approach. Our goal was not to provide a state-by-state directory of resources, but rather to give you a place to start in discovering what your state has to offer.

Chapter 3, about selling to the government, is included in the hope that it will encourage more women business owners to look seriously at often-overlooked opportunities in government contracting. The federal government and the states have a number of programs designed to encourage and assist women in this area.

The five chapters in this book are:

Chapter 1: Training, Technical Assistance and Counseling

This describes government and private resources offering all types of counseling, mentoring programs, specialized training, consulting, classes and seminars.

Chapter 2: Information Sources

Included here are offices, agencies, books, magazines and government publications where you can get practical information on a wide range of specific business topics.

Chapter 3: Selling to the Government

This is a primer on tapping into the huge market of state and federal governments, including specialized programs for women, publications, databases, and assistance centers.

Chapter 4. Membership Organizations

This is information on women's business and professional associations, and other general business organizations that offer educational and professional development opportunities.

Chapter 5. Program and Resource Listings

This is a list of telephone numbers, addresses and contacts for over 575 offices, programs and agencies referred to throughout the guide.

How To Use This Guide

We recommend that you skim the first four chapters, identifying the areas that interest you most. In some cases, contact information will be included with the program description, but in many cases you will need to use Chapter 5 to find phone numbers and addresses of the programs and organizations that interest you.

The Structure and Content

The five-part structure we used to present the information in this guide is designed to make it easy for you to get an overview of resources on particular topics. Long listings of agencies and offices are grouped in the last chapter for convenience. Once you know what you want to follow up on, it's easy to find the correct agency or program you want by using the cross references in the chapter you're reading or by using the *Quick-Find Guide* on the second page of Chapter 5.

We have made every effort to provide accurate and complete information on every listing. During the research phase, we requested and reviewed printed material from the programs and organizations we have included, and, in many cases, followed up the receipt of the material with phone calls to clarify information. Prior to publication, we verified all phone numbers and addresses to ensure that you spend as little time as possible looking for information and as much time as possible getting down to the business of building a successful enterprise.

Despite our efforts, phone numbers and addresses may have changed between the time we checked our data and the books came off the press. If you find incorrect information, please let us know by using the form at the end of this book.

Looking Ahead

We hope that each edition of this book will be bigger and better than the preceding one. As awareness grows for the unique needs and contributions of women entrepreneurs, more and more programs to serve this growing population will emerge. You can help us help other business women by sending us information about any program or organization that you would like to have considered for inclusion in future editions. We have included a form for directory submissions at the back of the book.

A Guide to Federal Agencies

The federal programs and resources described in this guide are made available by three key agencies:

- The Small Business Administration (SBA), including the SBA's Office of Women's Business Ownership
- The U.S. Department of Commerce
- The Women's Bureau of the U.S. Department of Labor.

The Small Business Administration (SBA)

The Small Business Administration is the only federal agency whose sole responsibility is to assist small businesses. It has been around for over 40 years, offering a cornucopia of free and low-cost assistance to small business owners throughout the country.

Of particular interest to women is the Office of Women's Business Ownership (OWBO). This office focuses on the special needs of women entrepreneurs and is described in more detail below.

The SBA is organized around a head office in Washington D.C. and a variety of regional, district and other field offices around the country. The field offices are really the workhorses of the agency, delivering services and programs customized to meet local and regional needs. Staff specialists in these offices— including a cadre of women's business representatives— are the ones who work directly with business owners, offering counseling, referring, problem-solving and education. In addition, SBA staff members in the field work with local and regional businesses and agencies to present seminars and workshops targeted to the needs of business owners in their area.

Contacting your regional office is a good way to start finding out about the SBA resources available to you. To locate the office that serves your area, see page 69.

The Office of Women's Business Ownership (OWBO)

OWBO is the place to call for just about any kind of business assistance you need. Geared to start-ups as well as stable and expanding businesses, the office serves as one-stop shopping for guidance, training, referral and information resources for women. OWBO does its job through a central office in Washington D.C. and a network of OWBO women's representatives located in SBA field offices across the country.

The office in Washington D.C. serves as a clearinghouse on women's business ownership issues at the federal level, and develops programs that are offered across the country through its network of women's representatives. The programs developed at the head office are designed to meet the special needs of business women in all areas and stages of business development.

The job of the nearly 70 women's representatives across the country is to help women become successful business owners by coordinating the head office's efforts out in the field. They customize programs to meet local needs, help women take advantage of programs and opportunities developed by the SBA, OWBO and other branches of the federal government, and steer women to appropriate local and state resources.

A call to the representative that serves your area is definitely worth the time. You'll undoubtedly come away with a list of appropriate people to call, agencies to contact and workshops to put on your calendar. To identify the representative in your area, see page 71.

For more information about the national OWBO office contact:

Small Business Administration
Office of Women's Business Ownership
409 Third St. SW, Sixth floor
Washington DC 20416
(202) 205-6673

Women's Bureau

The Women's Bureau is the only office in the federal government whose sole mission is to study issues of women and work. The office acts as an advocate for working women (including self-employed women) by disseminating information, working to change government policies and providing training and educational opportunities for women across the country through its network of 10 regional offices. To locate the regional office that serves your state, see page 89.

For more information about the national office, contact:

The Women's Bureau
U.S. Department of Labor
200 Constitution Ave. NW
Washington DC 20210
(202) 219-8913

U.S. Department of Commerce

A key function of the U. S. Department of Commerce is to help make federal resources available to the business community by providing information and assistance through its various bureaus such as the Minority Business Development Agency, the International Trade Administration, the Office of Business Liaison and the Office of Small and Disadvantaged Business Utilization. Commerce also initiates efforts to assure purchasing from women-owned businesses.

To get an overview of the Commerce Department and what it can do for you, request a Business Services Directory from:

U.S. Department of Commerce
Office of Business Liaison (OBL)
Herbert Hoover Building, Room 5898C
Washington DC 20230
(202) 482-3176
TDD (hearing impaired): (202) 482-4670 (This TDD number is not specifically for OBL, but by calling this number you will be directed to the appropriate person.)

1

Training, Technical Assistance and Counseling

Free, low-cost and specially designed training, counseling and technical assistance abound for women entrepreneurs. This section will help you find sources of:

- One-on-one counseling, including everything from a one-time session to long-term associations;

- Training, including classes, seminars, and workshops;

- Technical assistance, focusing on specific areas of business, such as financing, computer set-up, accounting, marketing and staffing.

The material in this chapter is organized in three categories: federal, state and private resources. Listings with a symbol next to them like the ones bordering the bottom of this page describe programs or resources that are specifically for women.

Other listed resources, while not for women only, offer excellent opportunities that you should not overlook.

We have included only brief references to sponsoring federal agencies so that you don't get bogged down in unnecessary details. For more information on them, see *A Guide to Federal Agencies*, on page viii.

A review of the definitions of common terms on page 127 may be helpful as you read this chapter.

Federal Resources

WNET Mentorship Program

- **A year-long program that matches successful businesswomen with owners of growing businesses**
- **Sponsored by: SBA's Office of Women's Business Ownership (OWBO)**

Wouldn't it be wonderful to have a successful, experienced businesswoman available for free advice and problem-solving every month for a year? OWBO has just such a program. Called the Women's Network for Entrepreneurial Training (WNET), it matches successful women entrepreneurs with owners of growing businesses in a year-long association.

The businesswoman, called a mentor, will meet with you about four hours each month for a year to give you advice and suggestions on just about any aspect of running your business. She serves as a coach, sounding board, guide, counselor, and critic, making a wealth of expertise, experience and savvy available to you. There is no charge to participate in the program, but you must:

- Have been in business at least one year
- Be ready to expand
- Demonstrate strong entrepreneurial skills
- Show potential for continued success
- Be willing to spend approximately four hours a month with your mentor
- Demonstrate a willingness to put into practice the advice you receive

To qualify as a volunteer mentor, a woman must:

- Have founded her own company
- Have been in business for at least five years
- Be willing to commit four hours a month for one year

How to Proceed

For information about WNET, contact your OWBO women's business ownership representative. (See page 71 to locate a representative in your area.)

Specialized Training Programs

- **Training in the areas of financing, procurement and international trade presented in series of regional seminars**
- **Sponsored by: The SBA's Office of Women's Business Ownership (OWBO)**

If you want to find out what it really takes to get a business loan, or how to take the plunge into international trade, OWBO's specialized training programs will interest you. Training sessions are customized to meet specific local needs by OWBO field representatives, using local sponsors and experts.

The trainings usually last one day, and fees vary (but are usually low). If the program is presented only by the SBA, it is often free. When other organizations or experts are involved in delivering the seminars, there may be a charge to attend.

Current topics include:

- Access to Capital
- Meet the Lender
- Selling to the Federal Government
- Women Going International (international trade)

How to Proceed

To receive information about upcoming conferences in your area, contact your local women's business ownership representative (see page 71), or, if you're handy with a computer and modem, check SBA Online (page 26) for dates and locations of upcoming seminars.

Women's Business Development Centers

- **Over 30 demonstration sites around the country that offer in-depth training and assistance**
- **Sponsored by: SBA's Office of Women's Business Ownership (OWBO)**

Thanks to OWBO, there are now over 30 women's entrepreneurial training centers across the country. These demonstration sites, set up to provide long-term local training and counseling, are private organizations with people qualified to train, counsel and guide women in finding capital, developing a business plan, setting up financial management systems, designing marketing programs and successfully managing a host of issues critical to business success.

These sites offer longer-term and more in-depth learning opportunities than OWBO's specialized training conferences. Services, training and costs are different at each demonstration site.

To give you an idea of the types of opportunities available at these training centers, we have profiled one site, the Women's Business Development Center (WBDC) in Chicago, which is the parent organization of three demonstration sites in Illinois. (Keep in mind that since each training site addresses local needs, specific programs will vary.)

Chicago's WBDC: What It Offers

WBDC is a place prospective, emerging and established women business owners can go to get comprehensive business training, personalized counseling and assistance for specific technical issues facing their businesses. The center serves as a Women's Business Enterprise (WBE) certification site, and, in conjunction with the certification program, offers specific workshops on how to win contracts in the public and private sector.

The center also offers a workshop series for prospective business owners, a four-week training program for women who have been in business more than 18 months, and short-term workshops on a variety of business management topics.

In conjunction with local colleges, WBDC offers business certificate programs for emerging and established business owners with a core curriculum in marketing, record-keeping, business law, insurance and business plan development. Its business finance program is designed to educate women about processes and sources of business financing, build skills in financial record-keeping, and provide personalized consulting on specific financial issues (such as on alternative financing) for women who have been denied conventional loans.

The center also sponsors an annual conference that features successful businesswomen as speakers.

How to Proceed

To find a demonstration site in your area, check the state-by-state listing on page 77. Training sites are not available in every state, but 11 new sites were added in 1993 and more will be added.

If there is not a site near you, check with OWBO headquarters periodically to find out if a new site is being added in your area. They can be contacted at:

Small Business Administration
Office of Women's Business Ownership
409 Third St. SW
Sixth Floor
Washington DC 20416
(202) 205-6673

SCORE Women's Business Counselors

- **Free counseling from retired women executives**
- **Sponsored by: Service Corps of Retired Executives (SCORE)**

SCORE provides free one-on-one counseling by a corps of volunteers nationwide. (The name is somewhat misleading: although most of the volunteers are retired, over 20% of them are employed full-time.) While SCORE runs a program open to all business owners, there is also a cadre of retired women executives, called Women's Business Ownership Coordinators, who specialize in advising women business owners.

SCORE tries to match a client's specific needs with a counselor who is experienced in a comparable line of business. Your counselor will help you identify and solve basic management problems as well as advise you on other business decisions. The counseling takes place either at your office or a SCORE chapter office.

How to Proceed

To find a women's SCORE counselor in your area, contact the women's business coordinator for your region from the list on page 85. Since these counselors change frequently, for the latest information contact the OWBO representative for your region from the list on page 71 or call the Washington D.C. office of the SBA's Office of Women's Business Ownership at (202) 205-6673.

To receive general SCORE counseling from any one of their counselors (not necessarily a woman), you can find local offices listed under SCORE in the white pages of your telephone book.

To receive more general information about SCORE services or to identify a SCORE counselor in your area, contact:

National SCORE Office
409 Third St. SW
Suite 5900
Washington DC 20416
(202) 205-6762

Small Business Institutes (SBIs)

- **Receive free consulting services by becoming a case study for qualified business students**
- **Sponsored by: The SBA**

Small Business Institutes provide free business consulting with a twist: the consultants are graduate and undergraduate business students who work under expert faculty guidance to help you solve management problems. This program gives students real-world experience—and gives you help with—specific business problems, like computerizing your accounting system, developing a personnel policy, starting a market study or designing a production plan.

The emphasis of the program is to help you find practical, realistic and affordable solutions to real problems or challenges facing your company. At the conclusion of the project, you will receive an oral presentation and a written report from the student, detailing a course of action.

According to SBA figures, more than 150,000 businesses and over 370,000 students from over 500 colleges and universities have benefited from the SBI program. To find out if there is an institute in your area, contact your regional SBA office (see page 69).

Small Business Development Centers (SBDCs)

- **A comprehensive program of counseling, workshops, classes and seminars at 700 centers around the country.**
- **Sponsored by: The SBA**

SBDCs, sponsored by the SBA and an educational or state or local government agency, offer one-stop shopping for business owners who need help. Any business owner—or prospective owner—can go to one of the nearly 700 centers around the country and get involved in pre-business workshops, one-on-one business counseling, classes and seminars on business startup, financing, management and marketing. Some SBDCs have long-term training programs for businesses in which a group of business owners go through a comprehensive program together that can last up to a year. People we have spoken with who have been through this program swear by it.

Counseling services are free; fees for seminars, classes, workshops and specialized training programs may be charged.

How to Proceed

To locate an SBDC in your area contact the SBDC director's office in your state (see page 80).

Business Information Centers (BICs)

- **Business resources and counseling at specialized information centers around the country**
- **Sponsored by: The SBA**

Need the latest market research data in your industry? Wish you had a computerized tutorial for that spreadsheet program you can't get the hang of? Need to talk with someone about a difficult personnel problem? Odds are you'll be able to find that—and a lot more—at a Business Information Center (BIC).

BICs offer a combination of high-tech business resources and one-on-one counseling from SCORE executives to help business owners increase their productivity and competitiveness. If you don't live close enough to a center to visit personally, assistance from online databases and phone counselors is still available. Face-to-face counseling may also be available to you even if you can't make it in to the center. The Seattle BIC, for example, sends SCORE counselors out on circuit rides to make their services more widely available.

Made possible through a partnership with private industry, BICs offer access to:

- Market research databases
- Online information exchange and research
- Interactive business training media
- Planning and spreadsheet software
- Video, print and CD-ROM libraries

How to Proceed

BICs are located in the SBA offices shown below. The phone numbers below will route you directly to the BIC, except in Atlanta.

- Atlanta: (404) 347-2441 (Push zero immediately to avoid hearing the tape, then ask to speak to a person who can route your call to the BIC.)
- St. Louis: (314) 539-6655
- Houston: (713) 773-6549
- Seattle: (206) 220-6527
- Los Angeles: (213) 251-7237

Assistance for Economically Disadvantaged Minorities: The 7(j) Program

- **Long-term technical assistance for economically disadvantaged minorities and socially and economically disadvantaged individuals**
- **Sponsored by: The SBA**

If you are one of the 400,000 or so minority women that the federal government estimates are also business owners, or if you are socially and economically disadvantaged, you may be eligible for up to nine years of free or low-cost technical assistance in accounting, marketing, proposal preparation and other specific issues in your industry.

This technical assistance is provided through the 7(j) Management and Technical Assistance Program, a special program for what the SBA designates as 8(a) businesses: businesses that can't compete effectively against businesses in their field because the owners don't have access to the same capital and credit opportunities as their competitors do.

The first step in taking advantage of the 7(j) program is to find out if you qualify as an 8(a) business. If you are Black, Hispanic, Native American or of Asian or subcontinent Asian (India, Pakistan, Nepal, etc.) descent, you are halfway there. These ethnic and racial minorities (and others that are periodically designated) are automatically considered socially disadvantaged. If you can also show economic disadvantage—and here the SBA considers both personal and business financial information in making a determination—you can become certified as an 8(a) firm.

If you do not belong to a group automatically considered socially disadvantaged, you may still qualify as an 8(a) firm if you can show a pattern of both economic and social disadvantage.

To apply for 8(a) certification you must fill out a detailed application and return it to an SBA office. Each application is considered on a case-by-case basis, and if approved you will be eligible for 7(j) assistance and other types of help through the SBA.

If you become 8(a) certified, contact the Business Opportunity Specialist in your district office's Minority Small Business Office to discuss your specific technical assistance needs. Also, if you have been in business in your area of specialization for at least one year and can provide a business service in accounting, marketing, or the other areas mentioned above, consider applying to the program to become a contracted provider to 7(j) firms. Most 7(j) providers are selected through a competitive process.

How to Proceed

For information about 7(j) or 8(a) certification, contact your regional SBA office (see page 69).

To receive information about becoming a provider and to be put on the SBA's Solicitation Mailing List contact:

Director: Division of Management and Technical Assistance
The Office of Procurement and Grants Management
U.S. Small Business Administration
409 Third St., SW
Fifth Floor
Washington DC 20416
(202) 205-6621

Training and Technical Assistance for Minorities

- **A national network of offices to provide technical assistance to all minority business owners**

- **Sponsored by: The U.S. Department of Commerce Minority Business Development Agency (MBDA)**

According to federal government figures, nearly 400,000 women business owners are also members of a minority group. If you're one of them, you are eligible for some specialized business assistance through the Minority Business Development Agency (MBDA).

The MBDA was set up by the Department of Commerce to foster the establishment and growth of minority-owned businesses. (Groups within the MBDA's definition of minority include Blacks, Puerto Ricans, Spanish-speaking Americans, American Indians, Eskimos, Aleuts, Asian-Pacific Americans, Asian Indians and Hasidic Jews.)

MBDA Services

The MBDA has six regional offices that oversee Minority Business Development Centers (MBDCs) in their area. The MBDCs—about 100 nationwide—are independent businesses or organizations (for-profit and non-profit private businesses, educational institutions, state and local agencies or Indian tribes) that receive partial funding from the MBDA to provide low-cost technical assistance to the minority business community. Each MBDC is staffed with business specialists who have expertise in:

- Business planning
- Marketing
- Financing
- Management counseling
- Bid estimation and bonding assistance for construction projects
- Procurement
- Franchising
- International trade

To give you an idea of what you can expect, we have profiled an MBDC in our area, Impact Business Consultants.

Impact Business Consultants

Impact offers a free initial consultation to discuss the nature of your business and the areas in which you need assistance. Based on that first meeting, a contract is drawn up specifying the work to be accomplished together.

Impact charges $10 an hour for their consulting services. Contracts can be for accomplishing specific tasks or to provide ongoing consulting services as needed. You can use Impact services on an ongoing basis or to help with particular issues periodically confronting your business. Since the MBDCs are private organizations, each one will work (and charge) a little differently.

Minority Enterprise Development Week (MED Week)

In observance of MED Week in September or October, the MBDA, in partnership with the SBA, sponsors activities across the country and in Washington D.C. to promote and acknowledge minority business ownership. Workshops, seminars, procurement trade fairs, recognition awards, networking events and other activities highlight MED Week celebrations.

How to Proceed

To locate the MBDC nearest you, call the regional MBDA office in your area (see page 87). Since MBDC locations change frequently, we have not included a listing for them.

For more general information about the MBDA, contact:

U.S. Department of Commerce
Minority Business Development Agency
Communications Division
Room 5073
Washington DC 20230
(202) 482-1936

For more information about MED Week contact:

U.S. Department of Commerce
MBDA/MED Week
Room H-6708
14th & Constitution Ave. NW
Washington DC 20230
(202) 482-5196

A Special Case: The Women's Bureau (U.S. Dept. of Labor)

- **A federal office set up specifically to study issues of women and work and to improve the status of working women, including self-employed women**

- **Sponsored by: The U.S. Department of Labor**

While the Women's Bureau does not offer standardized programs and services across the country as the SBA's Office of Women's Business Ownership does, we have included it because it and its regional offices offer some excellent resources for women entrepreneurs.

The bureau helps create opportunities for women by setting up demonstration programs, sponsoring educational events and providing information to policy-makers to influence their decisions about laws and programs for women.

The workhorses of the bureau are the 10 regional offices around the country in charge of delivering products and programs designed to meet local needs. To get an idea about what the regional offices do, we contacted the one in our area to find out the kinds of things it's done in the past several years. Keeping in mind that the different regions' activities vary, the following list of projects will give you an idea of what to expect:

- Development of a directory of blue-collar women-owned businesses
- Development of a women's small business referral resource
- Sponsorship of a Hispanic women's conference
- Sponsorship of a women-in-trades fair
- Sponsorship of a displaced homemakers conference

In other regions, there have been demonstration projects to help welfare recipients start micro-businesses and to extend unemployment benefits for women who wanted to go into business for themselves.

Each region also has discretionary funds to support small projects (like the development of the women-in-trades directory mentioned above) that will improve the status of women in their region. Individuals, groups, businesses and nonprofit organizations are all eligible to approach their regional office with project ideas.

The bureau also offers a variety of free publications about women and work, including a series of fact sheets on minority women's business ownership. Four separate fact sheets present statistics on Black, Hispanic, Asian American and Native Alaskan/American Indian women business owners.

How to Proceed

To find out more about the bureau's activities in your area, contact the regional office that serves your state (see page 89).

For more general information about the bureau and to receive the bureau's fact sheets, contact:

The Women's Bureau
U.S. Department of Labor
Room S 3317
200 Constitution Ave. NW
Washington DC 20210
(202) 219-8913

State Government Resources

Almost every state has at least one office which coordinates women's business ownership issues, and most states also have a variety of state, local, and privately sponsored programs. Since this directory has a national focus, we have not included detailed information on each state. Instead, we are providing key contacts and information resources to help you begin tapping in to your state and local programs.

These offices and other sources of useful information are included in Chapter 2 under State Resources. The membership organizations in Chapter 4 are also a valuable source of information on specialized topics.

Also, if you have not reviewed the sections on federal and private sources of training, counseling and technical assistance in this chapter, don't pass them by. You might be surprised to find out how many valuable federal and private programs are available in your area.

Training, Technical Assistance and Counseling

Private Resources

As more women start their own businesses and more appreciation develops for the unique challenges they face—as well as the special contribution they can make to how we do business in this country and abroad—more programs targeted to women will undoubtedly spring up. The resources in this section include non-profit and for-profit private organizations and companies that offer entrepreneurial and business learning opportunities on a national or regional basis. In addition to these listing, check:

- Chapter 4 for a listing of business associations. Most of them offer educational and professional development opportunities. Even if you do not want to join a particular group, you can often attend interesting workshops and seminars by asking to be put on the group's conference mailing list.

- The SBA-sponsored women's business development centers. These sites (described on page 3) are private organizations that receive partial funding through the SBA. The programs they offer are targeted to local needs, so check to see if there is a site in your area.

- The first-stop office in your state (see page 91). These agencies will have information about local and regional organizations that offer women's entrepreneurial training and counseling.

- Our companion publication, *Money Sources for Women Entrepreneurs*. Many organizations listed in it offer training and technical assistance in conjunction with microloan programs.

American Women's Economic Development Corp. (AWED)

■ **Entrepreneurial training with phone counseling outreach**

AWED offers fee-based personalized training, counseling and support services for women entrepreneurs in key areas of business operation (finance, accounting, marketing, design, planning, public relations, etc.). Telephone counseling and a telephone hotline make AWED resources available to women outside the New York City area who can not attend seminars and ongoing training programs.

AWED also has centers in Long Beach, California and Washington, D.C..

How to Proceed

For more information about AWED in general, contact the New York office at:

AWED
71 Vanderbilt Avenue, Suite 320
New York NY 10169
(212) 688-1900

Other centers can be reached at:

AWED
301 E. Ocean Blvd.
Suite 1010
Long Beach CA 90802
(310) 983-3750

AWED
1250 24th St., NW
Room 120
Washington DC 20037
(202) 857-0091

An Income of Her Own
■ **Entrepreneurial opportunities for teens and mothers**

Founded by Joline Godfrey, author of the best-selling book *Our Wildest Dreams*, this organization offers a variety of activities and opportunities to foster entrepreneurship in young women, including:

- A national business plan competition
- Summer camps to explore the excitement of entrepreneurship, including mother/daughter camps
- Membership benefits, including a newsletter and profiles of successful women entrepreneurs
- Entrepreneurship awareness conferences in your area designed to expose girls to successful business women

How to Proceed

The organization has an automated toll-free telephone system that plays short tapes you select using a touch-tone phone. Try calling first for an overview, although you can also fax or send for information.

An Income of Her Own
1169 Minnesota, # 7
San Jose CA 95125
(800) 350-2978
FAX: (805) 646-4206

Institute for Professional Business Women
■ **Low-cost seminars on topics of special interest to women**

The institute offers seminars around the country—or at your business location by special arrangement—targeted to the needs of professional and business women. For women working toward a degree, the seminars can also be used for Continuing Education units.

The Institute's reasonably priced seminars offer busy women a way to continue learning and to meet other professional women. They include a participant workbook, run from 9 a.m. to 4 p.m. and most cost $49 to $99 (some intensive seminars cost $195).

How to Proceed

Call or fax a request to be added to the institute's mailing list.

Institute for Professional Business Women
(A Division of Pryor Resources, Inc.)
P.O. Box 2951
Shawnee Mission KS 66201
(800) 255-6139
FAX: (913) 722-8585

National Businesswomen's Leadership Association

- **Low-cost seminars for women in business**

This association, affiliated with the Rockhurst College Continuing Education Center, offers seminars around the country designed to meet the special needs of women leaders and managers. Taught by experts in their fields, these one-day seminars offer busy women a tool for professional development and an opportunity to meet other women in business and management. Seminars range in price from $49 to $125, and include a participant workbook.

How to Proceed

Call to order a catalog of seminars and to be added to the mailing list.

National Businesswomen's Leadership Association
6901 West 63rd Street
P.O. Box 2949
Shawnee Mission KS 66201-1349
(800) 258-7246

National Chamber of Commerce for Women

- **Low-cost training, technical assistance and counseling for chamber members**

The chamber is a membership organization that makes a variety of resources and services available to working and self-employed women, for an annual fee of $96. Members participate in committees developed by the chamber to meet its members' needs. Committees include:

- The Business Owner's Advisory Taskforce, for women who own and run businesses located in commercial office space, retail stores and manufacturing facilities.

- The Home-Based Committee, for women who run businesses out of their homes or who work as independent contractors or free-lancers.

- The Productivity Improvement Network, which analyzes issues of gender difference in work and management styles, productivity incentives, quality controls, employee diversity and other productivity-related topics.

- The WOW (World of Women's) Business Committee, which provides assistance in the areas of micro-financing, imports and exports, international expansion, and letters of credit.

Assistance is provided primarily by:

- Hooking you up with a Committee Business Counselor who has expertise in your field. Counselors, who serve as free mentors for a period of time, are often available in your geographic area, but when one is not, you will be provided with a telephone counselor.

- Access to the resources and expertise of the chamber's information banks.

- Free workshops on business, work and self-employment issues. (If you cannot attend the workshops, you will receive a free manual.)

- Technical assistance on business plan development and finding financing.

Other services, and an introductory $25 membership, are also available.

How to Proceed

Call or write the chamber for an overview kit.

National Chamber of Commerce for Women
10 Waterside Plaza, Suite 6H
New York, NY 10010
(212) 685-3454

National Education Center for Women in Business

■ **Intensive learning opportunities for professional service providers, women business owners and young girls aspiring to entrepreneurship**

The center offers four main programs for aspiring and active women entrepreneurs:

- Strategy 2000: A two-day seminar addressing issues of women's business ownership as the turn of the century approaches, when it is anticipated that more than half the businesses in this country will be owned by women. The first day is for professional advisors (lawyers, accountants, etc.) to help them understand how to best serve women business owners. The second day is for business owners who want to grow or start their own businesses. By the end of 1994, this program should be available in 30 cities across the country.

- Camp Entrepreneur: A two-week camp for budding entrepreneurs, ages 6-12. It's a hands-on experience in business development that includes visits to businesses, use of computer simulations, budgeting, development of team skills, public speaking and more for young girls who are interested in the idea of business ownership. This camp will be made available across the country.

- Take Off: An intensive, personalized learning opportunity for successful business owners who are ready to take a growth step. Take Off is available in several locations around the country.

- Business Tours: International tours offer women business owners an opportunity to explore international markets with the guidance of an experienced businessperson who has conducted business in the tour area. Tours are currently planned to Italy, Czechoslovakia, Hungary, Mexico, Indonesia, Singapore and Australia. The tour program includes follow-up guidance after returning home.

- At Your Site: The center can schedule in-house presentations of its programs for your staff or clients.

- Campus Programs: The center offers classes, workshops and conferences at the Seton Hill campus and in the western Pennsylvania area on a variety of topics, including a special course for women who want to start a business or change the nature or structure of their existing business. Other topics include family business ownership, business ownership issues for women with disabilities, and women in high-tech businesses.

In addition to sponsoring conferences and workshops, the center publishes books, workbooks and videos, conducts research on women entrepreneurs and publishes a free newsletter. (For more information about these activities, see page 38).

How to Proceed

For more information about the center's activities and dates and locations of programs and tours, contact:

National Education Center for Women in Business
Seton Hill College
Seton Hill Dr.
Greensburg PA 15601-1599
(412) 830-4625 or (800) 632-9248

National Foundation for Women Business Owners (NFWBO)

- **Short-term intensive and ongoing learning opportunities for established and start-up business owners**

- **Sponsored by: NFBWO, a non-profit education fund founded by the National Association of Women Business Owners**

This foundation offers entrepreneurial training for owners of start-up and young businesses and leadership training programs for established women business owners. Its entrepreneurial training program, called EXCEL, combines intensive training sessions, ongoing mentoring and personalized counseling by qualified NFWBO chapter members

Costs for participation in the EXCEL program vary, depending on which chapter is offering it. Currently available in a limited number of sites around the country, NFWBO's goal is to expand the number of sites over time, eventually making the program available on a national basis.

NFWBO's leadership training is an intensive residential program in which 15 to 20 established women business owners attend a two-day seminar to fine-tune leadership skills, receive personalized guidance on key issues facing their companies and participate in personalized coaching sessions in media presentations and negotiating. The program, set up to maximize interaction between participants and provide opportunities to interact with leaders in management thinking, gives attendees a chance to engage in problem-solving sessions related to specific issues facing their businesses.

The curriculum changes yearly, offering new learning opportunities for women who want to return. The cost is about $1,800.

In addition to these specific training programs, NFWBO also is working to identify sources of capital for women business owners, and plans to develop workforce training and mentoring programs for the women's business community.

How to Proceed

Contact the national office for general information about NFWBO, the programs and to find out if the EXCEL program is available in your area.

National Foundation for Women Business Owners
1377 K Street, NW, Suite 637
Washington DC 20005
(301) 495-4975

Simmons Graduate School of Management

- **An MBA (Master's Degree in Business Administration) program that addresses women's special needs and interests**

Simmons offers the only MBA program in the country designed specifically for women. Founded by Margaret Hennig and Anne Jardim—co-authors of the 1974 bestseller *The Managerial Woman*—the school's curriculum adds to the traditional MBA program with course offerings on organizational management and gender differences.

Simmons seeks out a diverse student body. Students range in age from 24 to 55, average 10 years prior work experience and reflect educational backgrounds varying from pre-bachelor to doctoral level. Rather than select applicants only on the basis of what they bring to their participation in an MBA program—as many business schools do—Simmons looks at what the outcome of a woman's participation might be.

The one-year MBA program offers an opportunity to receive training in a field traditionally dominated by men—in the classroom and in the boardroom—by mastering all traditional subjects, gaining confidence in a supportive environment and learning specifically about gender issues that influence behavior and success in the business world.

How to Proceed

Contact the admissions office for an information packet.

Simmons College
Admissions Office
409 Commonwealth Avenue
Boston MA 02215
(617) 536-8390

Training, Technical Assistance and Counseling

Women's Commercial Funding

■ **Specialized help with financial management and free information resources**

The primary function of Women's Commercial Funding is to purchase accounts receivable from women business owners to help them maintain a positive, reliable cash flow. In addition, they offer a variety of business development opportunities as a service to the women's business community, including:

- Free technical assistance in developing effective business forms. The organization has business form templates that have stood the test of time which you can duplicate with your logo and company name.

- Free information on specific topics. They welcome questions from banks, professional women, service companies and organizations on issues of women's business ownership and access to capital.

- Training seminars on financial issues. The company has seminars on the drawing board designed for women business owners on credit and collections, accounts receivable and other financial management topics.

- A free resource library and referral service. (For more information about these services, see page 37.)

How to Proceed

As a division of Riviera Finance, Women's Commercial Funding has business development centers across the country where you can receive assistance. For a referral to an office in your area or information about specific services described above, contact one of the offices below:

- St. Louis: (800) 467-8214
- Atlanta: (800) 334-2092

A Woman's Education and Leadership Forum (WELF)

■ **Low-cost seminars foster self-esteem and business savvy**

WELF sponsors one-day conferences around the country on a variety of topics that help women acquire self-sufficiency, decision-making and personal success skills. Past conference workshops include *Self-Worth: Your Ultimate Power*, *Financial Management: Give Yourself Credit*, *How to Start and Manage Your Own Business*, *The Psychology of Winning* and a host of other topics specifically for women.

The organization's programs are based on a belief that self-esteem, self-confidence and self-knowledge are as critical to success as are specific skills. WELF tailors its conferences to local interests and concerns by surveying local women and working with local women's organizations and agencies.

Corporate sponsorships and contributions help keep conference attendance costs to a minimum, usually in the $35 to $45 range.

How to Proceed

Call or write for an information packet and for locations of upcoming conferences.

A Woman's Education and Leadership Forum
11781 Lee Jackson Hwy., Suite 190
Fairfax VA 22033
(703) 352-0551

Women's Information Bank (WIB)

■ **Technical assistance referral for women entrepreneurs**

WIB is an informal, international network of individuals who help educated women find business partners, start-up capital, and business incubator services. In addition to this technical business assistance, it coordinates the Thinking Women's Network, a network of female problem-solvers and authors around the world. It also maintains a library and placement services, conducts children's programs and offers computerized database services.

WIB publishes the *Thinking Women* newsletter and helps women find travel partners, work and educational opportunities and short-term housing and home exchanges in Washington and major cities around the world.

How to Proceed

Contact them at:

Women's Information Bank
3918 West Street NW
Washington DC 20007
(202) 338-8163

The Center for Family Business

■ **Specialized help for women in family-owned enterprises**

The Center for Family Business, founded and run by Leon and Katy Danco (a married couple) has been described by *Business Week* magazine as the "country's leading consulting firm for family companies." The center offers seminars and publications to address the special needs of owners who have inherited a business or who have set up their own companies as family enterprises.

The center offers an annual seminar, *Managing Succession Without Conflict*, which addresses issues critical to the success of the family-owned enterprise. The seminar is designed for all family members, even those who may not be active in the business but whose lives are affected by the way the business operates.

Key managers who are not family members are also encouraged to attend to learn about the dynamics of successful family-owned businesses. The three-day seminar, held once in the fall in Cleveland and once in the spring in Orlando, costs $1,795 for the first participant and $1,695 for all additional participants from the same business.

For business owners unable to attend the seminar, the center makes available a number of books written by the Dancos. *Inside the Family Business* and *Beyond Survival* discuss the unique issues facing family businesses and formulating effective strategies for successful management and succession. *From the Other Side of the Bed* by Judy Danco, looks at life in the family business from the woman's perspective.

How to Proceed

Contact the center at:

The Center for Family Business
5862 Mayfield Road
P.O. Box 24268
Cleveland OH 44124
(216) 442-0800

The Family Business Program

■ **Seminars, workbooks and family camp for owners of family-owned businesses**

Founded by nationally recognized speaker, researcher and consultant Patricia Frishkoff, The Family Business Center offers seminars (primarily in the Pacific Northwest), workbooks and a newsletter on family business ownership issues. Seminars cover communications, teamwork, succession and ownership transition. A summer family camp is also offered. The program's workbooks, *The Succession Survival Kit* and *Preparing...Just in Case* help families address issues of the transition process. The quarterly *Family Business Newsletter* includes case histories, articles and national news about family business issues.

How to Proceed

Contact the program at:

Family Business Program
College of Business
Oregon State University
Bexell Hall, Room 201
Corvallis OR 97331-2603
(503) 737-3326

National Business Incubation Association (NBIA)

■ **Support and technical assistance for start-ups**

Business incubators are facilities set up to provide small start-up enterprises with affordable space, support services and business development services, such as marketing, financing and business management. The five-year success rate for businesses that locate in incubator facilities is much higher than that for other small businesses (80% compared to 62%). There are over 500 incubators in the United States and it is projected that this successful phenomenon will grow, making incubator facilities available in more and more communities.

How to Proceed

To locate an incubator in your area, contact the NBIA at:

National Business Incubation Association
One President Street
Athens OH 45701
(614) 593-4331

Private Seminar Providers

■ A seminar smorgasbord at reasonable prices

The companies listed here deliver reasonably priced ($50 to $100 per day) seminars around the country on a variety of management and business issues. Typical topics include customer service, total quality management, team-building, communications skills, stress management and employee relations.

How to Proceed

Call the organizations below to be put on their mailing lists.

CareerTrack
3085 Center Green Dr.
Boulder CO 80301
(800) 334-6780

Fred Pryor Seminars
P.O. Box 2591
Shawnee Mission KS 66201
(800) 255-6139

Key Productivity Center
P.O. Box 27-480
Kansas City MO 64180
(800) 821-3919

SkillPath Inc.
6900 Squibb Road
P.O. Box 2768
Mission KN 66201
(800) 873-7545

2
Information Sources

Business success is often an information game. Knowing what to do, who to contact and how to locate the information you need all play a critical role in making sound business decisions.

This chapter provides more general resources to help you find out just about anything you need in the business arena. Included are:

- State and federal offices that can provide information directly or refer you to an appropriate office or individual.

- Private and government books and publications on just about any business issue you can imagine.

- Private organizations offering business resource and referral services.

In addition to the listings in this chapter, the membership organizations in Chapter 4 are excellent sources for information targeted to your individual needs and interests.

The material in this chapter is organized in three categories: federal, state and private resources. We have included only brief references to sponsoring federal agencies so that you don't get bogged down in unnecessary details. For more information on them, see *A Guide to Federal Agencies* on page viii.

Listings with a symbol like the ones bordering the bottom of this page are exclusively for women.

Federal Resources

Office of Women's Business Ownership (OWBO)

- Information specifically for and about women business owners
- Sponsored by: The SBA's Office of Women's Business Ownership

In addition to sponsoring a variety of training and technical assistance programs and a national network of women's business representatives, this office makes available a number of valuable publications.

You can get started taking advantage of OWBO's resources by requesting the free publication *For Women: Managing Your Own Business*. This book is a clear and comprehensive guide to issues involved in starting and running your own business. The book begins with a discussion of personal issues to consider when planning for business ownership. It then goes on to cover key topics on business management, including business planning, accounting, marketing, legal issues, personnel management and more.

Practical and informative, the book also includes some worksheets and a glossary of business terms. A statistical report about women in business is also available from OWBO.

For more information about OWBO or to receive copies of these publications, call or write:

SBA Office of Women's Business Ownership
409 Third St. SW
Sixth Floor
Washington DC 20416
(202) 205-6673

National Women's Business Council (NWBC)

- A special council that studies issues related to women's business ownership
- Sponsored by: The U.S. Government

NWBC was established by the Women's Business Ownership Act of 1988 to study the status of women business owners. The councils studies four key issues related to women's business ownership:

- Availability of data about women-owned businesses and how data is collected
- The role federal, state and local governments play in fostering women's business ownership

- The status of women in business and women-owned businesses nationally, including progress made and barriers that remain to full participation in the mainstream of the American economy

- Government initiatives on women-owned businesses, including procurement

The council holds hearings, receives evidence and reports its findings annually to the president and the Congress. It also makes recommendations for policy and legislation.

For information about the office and its reports, contact:

The National Women's Business Council
409 Third St., SW
Suite 7425
Washington DC 20024
(202) 205-3850

SBA Publications and Videotapes

- **Low-cost publications on running and starting a business available by mail**
- **Sponsored by: The SBA**

The ABCs of Borrowing, Understanding Cash Flow, Small Business Decision-Making, and *Managing Employee Benefits* are just a few of the titles of publications you can order from the SBA for a dollar or less. Also available are videotapes about exporting, business planning and business promotion that cost $30 each. To order a directory of publications and an order form, contact:

SBA Publications
P.O. Box 30
Denver CO 80201-0030
or call (202) 205-7418 from 10 a.m. to 3 p.m. EST.

Small Business Administration Answer Desk

- **Make a toll-free call for recorded information about SBA programs or to speak with a business expert**
- **Sponsored by: The SBA**

This is a toll-free telephone line to the SBA office in Washington D.C.. You can call and listen to any of several short recorded messages describing various programs, and afterwards you can speak to a small business advisor directly, if you wish.

The recorded message directs you to several short tapes which you can select by using buttons on your touch-tone phone. (If you don't have a touch-tone phone, just stay on the line, and you'll get help.)

The messages available include:

- Starting your own business

- Financing your business
- Counseling and training
- SBA services and local assistance
- Minority business information
- Veteran's affairs
- Women's business ownership
- International trade
- Procurement assistance

After you've listened to a message, if you press 3, you can speak to a live person who can help with any questions you might have. Unfortunately, you can't just speak to a person when you call. You have to listen to a recording first, and then press 3 at the end.

Here are a few tips for using this service:

- The recordings tell you that you can interrupt some messages *at any time* with another selection, but this doesn't always work. Sometimes you'll have to wait until the present message ends before you can make any selection.
- Be quick with your selection as soon as the message ends, or all you'll hear is "Thanks for calling the SBA" and the line will go dead.
- If the system doesn't work properly, and you can't seem to get anyone on the line (which happened to us several times), call back and immediately press 0 several times as soon as the first recording starts. This isn't an official option, but it will usually get you to a human voice who can help you.

How to Proceed

Call (800) 827-5722. Have a pencil and paper handy to jot down the numbers of the pre-recorded tapes you're interested in.

For TDD (hearing-impaired), the number is (202) 205-7333.

SBA Online

- **An online computer database of SBA services, programs and representatives**
- **Sponsored by: The SBA**

If you have a computer and a modem, the SBA's online computer bulletin board can be an excellent resource for up-to-date information on current programs, seminars, local resources, and other government information services. (We used this service frequently when compiling this directory.)

Using an easy-to-follow series of menus, you can access information and download files on every aspect of the SBA, including application forms for financial and procurement services. And there's a special area for details of programs, seminars, agencies and human resources in your local area.

The best way to use this service is to just browse through the menus and explore what's available. You have up to two hours per call, so don't feel rushed.

One tip: You can download a list of all the files available on the system, and view it or print it out in your word processor. The file name is SBAFILES.TXT, and takes just a couple minutes to download.

Because use was so heavy during the service's first year, when all services were available on the toll-free line donated by Sprint International, a new toll 900 number has been added. While you can still view and download all files related to the SBA and the government, other computer software that was formerly available using the toll-free number can now only be downloaded using a 900 number. When calling this number, you're given access to IBM and Macintosh computer software libraries which contain over 100 programs that have been put on the service for users to download and run. You'll find software on everything from writing a business plan to spreadsheet templates and tax return preparation programs. It's well worth looking through.

The 900 number also gives you access to a mail service and connections to other government bulletin boards, including the National Technical Information Service, which shares results of government-sponsored research.

How to Proceed

Call (800) 697-4636 for 9600 baud modems, or (800) 859-4636 for 2400 baud modems. On your first call, you'll be asked to enter your name, city and state. You'll also need to choose a password (and remember it). You can call 24 hours a day.

The toll number is (900) 463-4636. The cost is $.30 for the first minute, and $.10 for each additional minute, so a half-hour session is only $3.20, which isn't bad. Other online services, like CompuServe, normally charge between $8 and $16 per hour for similar downloading time.

Business Information Centers (BICs)

- **Business information available in centers around the country**
- **Sponsored by: The SBA**

Located in district offices around the country, Business Information Centers (BICs) offer the latest high-tech resources in market research and business training and counseling. (For more information about the full range of services offered, see page 6.) Made possible through a partnership with private industry, BICs offer access to:

- Market research databases
- Online information exchange and research
- Interactive business training media
- Planning and spreadsheet software
- Video, print and CD-ROM libraries

How to Proceed

BICs are located in the SBA offices below. These numbers get you straight to the BIC, except in Atlanta where you'll go through a switchboard.

- Atlanta: (404) 347-2441 (Press 0 to avoid the recorded loop and speak directly to an operator.)
- St. Louis: (314) 539-6655
- Houston: (713) 773-6549
- Seattle: (206) 220-6527
- Los Angeles: (213) 251-7237

Office of Business Liaison (OBL)

- **Get help navigating through the maze of the federal agencies, programs and requirements**
- **Sponsored by: The U.S. Department of Commerce**

Do you have a business-related question that you think the federal government can answer, but don't even know who to call? If you do, then the Office of Business Liaison in the U.S. Department of Commerce is the place to start. It has specialists available to answer your questions on government policies, programs and services.

OBL staff will be able to provide the information you need (or find someone who can) on topics including procurement, marketing, statistical sources and regulatory matters. OBL specialists maintain a network with other federal agencies so they can also help you with questions that fall outside the scope of the Department of Commerce.

Also available is a handy 35-page booklet called the *Business Services Directory*. It's free and packed with information on federal agencies, including quick-reference phone numbers and addresses.

How to Proceed

To order a booklet or to speak with an OBL specialist, contact:

U.S. Department of Commerce
Office of Business Liaison
Herbert Hoover Bldg.
Room 5062
Washington DC 20230
(202) 482-3176

TDD (hearing-impaired): (202) 482-4670. This is the main departmental TDD number. Once you call here, someone will patch you through to an appropriate person.

Federal Information Centers

- **More help in dealing with the federal bureaucracy**
- **Sponsored by: The U.S. government**

Federal Information Centers were set up to help citizens with questions about the federal government to get off the referral merry-go-round. Specially trained and selected staff will answer your questions directly or find the appropriate person for the job. You can write or call with your request.

How to Proceed

Send written requests to:

Federal Information Center
P.O. Box 600
Cumberland MD 21502

There is also a list of toll-free numbers for regional offices on page 115 . If you can't locate an appropriate number, call (301) 722-9098. For TDD (hearing-impaired), call (800) 326-2996.

U.S. Government Printing Office

- **Books, pamphlets and other publications on all aspects of business.**

The federal government is a source of low-cost books on marketing, procurement, accounting, taxation and many other topics.

How to Proceed

To order a free catalog of business books, write to:

Free Business Catalog
U.S. Government Printing Office
Stop SM
Room 1114
Washington DC 20402

The printing office publishes more than 15,000 books, pamphlets, posters and other government publications on topics ranging from labor relations to census data. To receive information about these publications, request a catalog of U.S. Government books and a subject bibliography index from:

Superintendent of Documents
U.S. Government Printing Office
Washington DC 20402

The Government Printing Office also offers access to government information and publication ordering through an electronic bulletin board. For more information about the printing office's Electronic Information Dissemination Services, call (202) 512-1526 or fax (202) 512-1262.

In addition to the offices in Washington D.C., there are over 20 government bookstores located across the country. These stores are open to the public for direct purchases or to order government publications for you from the Government Printing Office. For the locations and phone numbers of these stores, see page 116.

GAIN Information Service

■ Interactive fax system gives you federal facts fast

Would you like to get an up-to-date list of federal contracts for services or products your company can supply? Or find out any time about current federal loans or grants you might be eligible for? Now, thanks to the Government Access & Information Network (GAIN) you can.

GAIN, run by the private company DynamicFAX in Rockford, Illinois, is an electronic database and interactive fax system that leads you through the federal information maze to help you find just the information you're looking for. This interactive fax system targeting small business, including minority and women-owned businesses, provides instant information about federal contracts, loans, grants and technical assistance. Then, when you've found it, the system transmits the information directly to your fax (or any other fax you designate). It's fast, current and easy to use.

How to Proceed

To tap into the GAIN system you can dial in on either an 800 or 900 line. If you use (800) 876-4246, you'll have to punch in a credit card number, and your faxed documents will be billed to your credit card at $3.50 each.

If you use (900) 990-4246, instead of getting a bill through your credit card, a charge of $2.25 a minute (average calls run four minutes) will show up on your phone bill.

State Resources

First-Stop Offices

■ **The place to start in your state**

Since all states' programs vary, we've coined the term *first-stop office* to mean the place to start to find out about procurement, conferences, training, special programs and financing in your state. Some of the offices will be set up to provide services and some will not, but all will be able to at least provide referral services to appropriate agencies.

To give you an idea of the types of activities or resources you can expect to find, we've profiled two first-stop offices below.

The Office of Minority, Women and Emerging Small Business (Oregon)

This first-stop office in Oregon is a state-funded agency set up to help women business owners in several ways. It operates as a referral and resource agency, providing a packet of information about agencies a woman needs to contact when starting a business (like the Secretary of State's Corporation Division to register a trade name) and a packet of information about looking for business financing in her state. In addition to the packets and general referral services, the office also refers women to sources of business counseling in their area.

The office runs the state's WBE certification program, allowing women business-owners to take advantage of a variety of contracting opportunities. In conjunction with the certification program, it publishes a directory of the WBE-certified businesses.

This directory is used by private and public purchasing agents to identify companies that can fulfill their organization's needs for services and products. To help women become certified, the office sponsors workshops and training sessions on certification procedures.

PROFILE

Women's Business Development Corporation (Maine)

Since there is not a designated state agency to promote women's business ownership in Maine, the role is played by the Women's Business Development Corporation (WBDC), a private nonprofit organization funded in part through the State Department of Economic and Community Development and the Department of Transportation. As the first-stop office in Maine, it provides a comprehensive program of advocacy, referral and education.

WBDC works to effect state and federal economic policy and build awareness of the social and economic contributions of women-owned businesses. As a referral agency, the corporation is staffed with specialists familiar with state resources who can send women with specific business-related concerns or questions to the right place.

As an educational organization, it offers women a comprehensive program of management and technical assistance. It sponsors regular workshops on sales, marketing, financial planning and other topics at its main site, and sets up regular regional meetings around the state to provide training, support and networking opportunities.

Its annual state conference includes a trade show and workshops, along with additional opportunities for women to network and gather information about business opportunities. A mentorship program is available to help new and emerging businesswomen strengthen existing skills and learn new ones needed for business growth.

The organization also publishes a variety of materials including a newsletter, a membership directory, a state directory of women-owned businesses and a business workbook.

How to Proceed

Contact the first-stop office listed for your state (see page 91).

National Association of Women's Business Advocates (NAWBA)

- **A network of state government representatives and independent business women working to improve opportunities for women business owners**

This association is made up of advocates across the country who work on a state level to advocate for women business owners and to assist states in implementing useful programs for the women's business community. The advocates meet semi-annually to share information about successful programs and activities. Described as a state-to-state mentoring program, NAWBA is helping ensure that more and more states recognize and support their women business owners.

Advocates are knowledgeable about programs, legislation and policies on a state and national level that affect businesswomen. About 20 states are represented in the association.

How to Proceed

To see if there is a women's business advocate in your state who can steer you toward useful resources or bring you up to date on policy and legislation that may effect you, see the state-by-state listing on page 118. For more general information about NAWBA, contact:

Melody K. Boucher
NAWBA
c/o Ohio Department of Development
P.O. Box 1001
Columbus OH 43215
(614) 466-4945

Women's Business Resource Program

- **One quick call gives you up-to-date information on who to contact about business resource programs in your state**

The Women's Business Resource Program, sponsored by the state of Ohio's Department of Development, has a compiled a state-by-state electronic database and printed directory of business resource programs and offices. Anyone can call in and get names, addresses and phone numbers of people and programs to contact.

Information is not restricted to programs that assist only women business owners, so you will get a good cross section of business assistance opportunities in your state, including those designed for women only. Their printed directory provides information about the key contact office in each state responsible for coordinating women's business issues.

How to Proceed

For more information about the program or to request information about your state's programs, contact:

Women's Business Resource Program, SBDC
Ohio Department of Development
P.O. Box 1001
Columbus OH 43215
(800) 848-1300
(614) 466-4945

State Executive Directory Annual

- **A directory of state-by-state listings of government offices and agencies**
- **Published by Carroll Publishing Co.**

This directory provides state-by-state listings of all governmental offices and agencies, including those involved in business development. To locate appropriate agencies, check your state's headings for Department of Commerce and Department of Economic Development. Each state is organized differently with different agencies and activities, but under these two headings you will find such agencies as Office of Business Development, Women in Business and Community and Business Development.

How to Proceed

Most public libraries have this book in the reference section. If yours doesn't, ask the reference librarian if it is available on interlibrary loan. Also, tell the librarian what kind of information you're looking for; he or she will probably know some other ways to locate it for you.

You may also contact the publisher directly at:

Carroll Publishing Co.
1058 Thomas Jefferson St. NW
Washington DC 20007
(202) 333-8620

State Blue Books

- **State directories cover offices, agencies and programs involved in business assistance**

- **Published by individual state governments**

Almost all states publish a directory of their government offices, agencies and programs. These directories may have different titles in different states, but they will provide you with information similar to that found in the *State Executive Annual* (above), except the information will be more detailed and will include additional information about special state and local programs.

How to Proceed

Ask your local reference librarian for the title of this publication in your state.

The States and Small Business: A Directory of Programs and Activities

- **State-by-state listings of small business-related offices, programs and legislation**

- **Published by: U.S. Government Publications Office**

This provides information about each state's legislative activities and business offices and programs that affect small-business development. There is also information about state loan programs, procurement and regulatory assistance, special programs for targeted groups (like minorities) and industries (like high-tech), and trade and export assistance. The latest edition of this book was published in 1990, so some of the listings may be outdated.

How to Proceed

The directory may be available in your local library, or you can buy it for $12 from:

Superintendent of Documents
U.S. Government Printing Office
Washington, DC 20402

To place a credit card order call (202) 783-3238 or FAX to (202) 512-2250. The publication order number is 045-000-00260-8.

Private Resources

The Women's Information Resource Exchange (WIRE)

■ An online service for and about women

This is an online computer service just for women that includes conferences on health and fitness, political issues, careers, finance, parenting and more. It also includes a forum for women business owners called the Business Roundtable. Designed to be user-friendly, the service uses a point-and-click interface, phone support and a Big Sister program for new subscribers to provide help when necessary. In addition to the many forums available, the service holds an open online discussion for all subscribers every Wednesday evening. The monthly subscription rate is $17.

How to Proceed

Contact WIRE at the address below for a brochure or a start-up kit that includes software, access information and a user manual.

WIRE Networks Incorporated
435 Grand Ave.
Suite D
S. San Francisco CA 94080
(415) 615-8989 or (800) 210-9999

Marketing to Women

■ A market research newsletter provides data about women

If you offer a service or product specifically for women, or if you want to find out what women are looking for, this publication may be for you. *Marketing to Women* is a monthly newsletter that reports market research data on women and their buying habits in an understandable, concise format. Each month staff members review approximately 90 research studies, gather reports from all market major research firms (like Gallup, Neilsen and others), and review articles from an online database of over 650 publications. From eating habits to reading habits and just about everything in between, this newsletter can provide you with critical information in designing an effective program to market to women.

How to Proceed

Contact *Marketing to Women* at the address below:

Marketing to Women
33 Broad St.
Boston MA 02109
(617) 723-4337

National Association of Women's Yellow Pages

■ **A woman-to-woman advertising network**

The Women's Yellow Pages is a directory (modeled after the phone company yellow pages) of women business owners in a particular state or area. Business owners pay to advertise, and businesses and individuals purchase the directory as a reference publication. This is an excellent way for women to get the word out about their products and services and to learn about other women-owned businesses they might want to patronize.

For women interested in becoming Yellow Pages publishers, there is help through the national office. A $300 initiation fee provides a new publisher with a mentor in her area, training opportunities, attendance at the national conference and use of the national logo.

How to Proceed

To find out if there is a directory in your area, see page 125. For more general information and to investigate the possibility of starting a Women's Yellow Pages in your area, contact:

The National Association of Women's Yellow Pages
7358 Lincoln Ave.
Suite 150
Chicago IL 60646
(708) 679-7800

Women's Commercial Funding

■ **This company offers free information on financial topics and issues of women's business ownership**

The primary function of Women's Commercial Funding is to purchase accounts receivable from women business owners to help them maintain a positive, reliable cash flow. In addition, they offer a variety of business development opportunities, and serve as an information resource to the women's business community by:

- Answering inquiries from banks, professional women, service companies and membership organizations on issues of women's business ownership and access to capital.

- Making information from its resource library available for free. Women can call in with questions and get answers right on the phone or have material sent by mail.

- Providing phone referrals from its database of women professionals, business owners and organizations around the country. This database is an ongoing project which Women's Commercial Funding adds to regularly.

(For more information about technical assistance and training from this organization, see page 19.)

How to Proceed

Contact Women's Commercial Funding at one of the toll-free numbers below:

- St. Louis: (800) 467-8214
- Atlanta: (800) 334-2092

National Education Center for Women in Business (NECWB)

■ Leading edge information on women business owners

NECWB, a women's entrepreneurial training, research and resource center, makes information about entrepreneurship for women available in a number of ways (see page 16 for information about the center's training activities):

- The center conducts ongoing research that examines issues of women (including young adults and children) and business ownership. Currently, the center is coordinating a multi-phase research project on the management styles of women in business. Results from the study will be used to educate corporations about how they can benefit from women's natural management style, and will provide the groundwork for planning business school curricula that will attract women applicants.

- A 900 line which will allow people to call in for information and referrals is planned for startup in 1994.

- The center's free newsletter, *The Source*, provides general information about women in business and keeps readers updated on the center's seminars, research and other activities.

- They publish books, reports videos and workbooks on women's business ownership issues. Some current titles include *Women Entrepreneurs in Action* (video), *The Women Entrepreneur* (research report), *Women and Family Business* (article reprints) and *The ABCs of Business for Children*.

How to Proceed

For information about center activities and resources, contact the center at:

The National Center Education Center for Women in Business
Seton Hill College
Seton Hill Drive
Greensburg PA 15601-1599
(800) 632-9248
(412) 830-4625

National Foundation for Women Business Owners (NFWBO)

■ NFWBO Leadership Institute gathers and disseminates data on women business owners

NFWBO initially teamed up with Cognetics, Inc. to develop the first comprehensive database of information on women's business ownership in this country.

The database contains the results of surveys of the membership of The National Association of Women Business Owners and surveys of women business owners across the nation. With it, the foundation can make a wide range of valuable information on women-owned businesses available. In conjunction with The National Association of Women Business Owners, NFWBO also offers specialized training programs for women business owners (for more information, see page 17). The project's first publication, *Women-Owned Businesses: The New Economic Force*, is an informative, lively and inspiring mix of statistics and profiles of successful businesswomen.

How to Proceed

Contact NFWBO at the address below to order a specific publication or to request a list of current publications.

National Foundation of Women Business Owners
1377 K. St., NW
Suite 637
Washington DC 20005
(301) 495-4975

Barbara Brabec Productions

■ **Help for the aspiring or established home-based business owner**

Barbara Brabec is an established home-based entrepreneur who offers advice, information and inspiration through her books, reports, newsletter and telephone consulting. Brabec publishes a quarterly report called the *National Home Business Report*, a variety of reports on home-based business issues, and she and is the author of the how-to guide and directory *Homemade Money*. Recognized as a national authority on the subject, Brabec's materials on home-based business operation are practical and informative.

How to Proceed

For more information and to receive a *Home Business Success Catalog*, contact:

Barbara Brabec Productions
P.O. Box 2137
Naperville IL 60567
(708) 717-0488

Books For and About Women in Business

■ **A get-started list of good reading material**

Vision, inspiration and a large supply of nuts and bolts to help with the success of daily operations are all yours for the reading. Books on marketing, management, financing, and communication, along with stories of other women's successes, challenges and failures, can go a long way toward keeping you inventive, effective and motivated.

To limit our listing to current information, we have included only those books published after 1987 that were written specifically for or about women. There are certainly lots of good books about women in business published before 1988, as well as many good general books on business startup and management.

This list though, while not comprehensive, provides a good starting point for the women business owner who is looking for information, encouragement and ideas. The bibliographies in the books listed here can also be a valuable resource in locating other general business books and books on specialized topics.

How to Proceed

Many of these books are available in your local library or bookstore. If not, contact the publisher to order directly or find out where the book is carried in your area.

Body and Soul: Profits with Principles; The Amazing Success Story of Anita Roddick
Anita Roddick
Crown Publishing Group, 1991
New York NY
(800) 726-0600

An inspiring success story that proves business can succeed without following the old maxims. It shows how business practice can foster social change and environmental responsibility.

The Entreprenerial Women's Guide to Owning A Business
Entrepreneur, 1992
(800) 421-2300

A comprehensive guide (at the hefty price of almost $90) that addresses the basics for prospective and current business owners. Covers all phases of business start-up from analyzing your readiness, researching your business idea, writing a business plan, getting capital, going to market and more.

Exceptional Entrepreneurial Women: Strategies for Success
Russel Taylor
Greenwood Publishing, 1988
Westport CT
(203) 226-3571

An analysis of how and why 15 prominent women entrepreneurs successfully grew their companies to over $10 million in annual sales. Based on in-depth interviews, the book examines issues facing women business owners, including special problems, strategies for success and common traits shared by the interviewees.

From the Other Side of the Bed
Katy Danco
The Center for Family Business, 1991
Cleveland OH
(216) 442-0800

Written by a woman who has worked with thousands of women involved in family-owned businesses, this book offers insight into business and personal needs of women in family enterprises.

Information Sources

The International Businesswomen of the 1990s: A Guide to Success in the Global Marketplace
Marlene Rossman
Greenwood Publishing, 1990
Westport CT
(203) 226-3571

This book examines how women's socialization as cooperative team players opens a world of business opportunity in the changing global economy.

Hers: The Wise Women's Guide to Starting a Business on $2,000 or Less
Carol Milano
Allworth Press, 1991
New York NY
(212) 777-8395

A practical book that covers the nuts and bolts of starting a good business on a shoestring. It includes how to decide what business to go into, how to decide if entrepreneurship is for you, how to research the viability of your idea and how to get to the point where you're ready to open. Profiles of women who have done it on a shoestring add interest and credibility to the approach.

Keys for Women Starting and Owning a Business
Carole Sinclair
Barron, 1991
Hauppauge NY
(516) 434-3311

This book looks at special issues of being a women in business, including financing, discrimination, special opportunities for women, working effectively with men and building supportive relationships with other women.

On Your Own: A Woman's Guide to Building a Business
Laurie Zuckerman
Upstart Publishers, 1990
Dover NH
(800) 235-8866

This is a comprehensive discussion of personal and business issues involved in business ownership, including how to set up a support network, develop (and use) a business plan, analyze your market and manage your finances.

Our Wildest Dreams: Making Money, Having Fun, Doing Good
Joline Godfrey
Harper Collins, 1992
New York NY
(800) 242-7737

Here's an informative, inspiring account of one woman entrepreneur's developing awareness of how women business owners are perceived and treated in our society. It includes success stories, resources and a wealth of good ideas about what needs to happen to improve the status of women business owners.

The Female Advantage
Sally Helgesen
Doubleday, 1990
New York NY
(800) 223-6834

This is an in-depth examination of leadership based on studies of women in leadership roles. Includes case studies of four successful women leaders.

Hardball for Women: Winning at the Game of Business
Pat Heim (with Susan Golant)
Lowell House, 1992
Los Angeles CA
(310) 552-7555

This book examines the unwritten rules of business in a culture where men learn to play the game early on. Offering practical strategies for overcoming the disadvantages of a late start, it's designed to help women become successful players in the business arena. A series of situations and solutions in the authors' companion book, *The Hardball for Women Playbook*, provides an opportunity to practice applying the ideas in a no-risk environment.

What Mona Lisa Knew: A Women's Guide to Getting Ahead in Business by Lightening Up
Barbara Mackoff
Lowell House, 1991
Los Angeles CA
(310) 552-7555

A compelling look at why being too serious can keep you from getting ahead. Sprinkled with accounts of the author's own experience, anecdotes about other women and research data, this book offers practical strategies for lightening up making the power of humor work for you. It covers how humor can be used to more effectively manage others, work with men and cultivate a happy home life.

A Women's Guide to Starting a Small Business
Mary Lester
Pilot Books, 1989
Babylon NY
(516) 422-2225

This is a guide to developing a low-overhead service business, with a 20-point beginners checklist.

Woman to Woman: Street Smarts for Women Entrepreneurs
Geraldine Larkin
Prentice Hall, 1993
Englewood Cliffs NJ
(800) 233-1360

Woman to Woman is a fast track for entrepreneurs who want to do it right the first time around. Written by a seasoned entrepreneur and women's business trainer, this book lets you learn from the author's frank discussion of her own mistakes and the mistakes of her clients. Covering all the practical aspects of business—from inception and financing to marketing and management—it also includes chapters on family involvement in your business, retirement planning and how to live a happy healthy life and still be successful.

Woman's Guide to Starting a Business
Claudia Jessup and Genie Chipps
Henry Holt and Company, 1991
New York NY
(800) 488-5233

This is a four-part guide to getting started, surviving and thriving as a business owner, including a blueprint for effective planning, a startup guide, profiles of successful women entrepreneurs and a resource section.

Women Entrepreneurs: 33 Personal Stories of Success
Linda Pinson and Jerry Jinnett
Upstart Press, 1993
Dover NH
(800) 235-8866

A diverse group of women business owners tell their stories about getting started, overcoming hardship, and serving as role models for others. History and statistics about women in business, as well as a resource directory, are included.

Women in Business
Ronya Kozmetsky
Gulf Publishing, 1989
Houston TX
(713) 520-4480

This book of case studies illustrates how women's managerial styles contribute to the growth of their companies. The book examines both corporate and entrepreneurial contexts, looking at issues related to business growth, balancing family and business, raising capital and hiring support professionals.

Magazines for Women and Entrepreneurs

■ Regular installments of ideas, information and inspiration

When you're busy just trying to make it through each day or week, getting a regular dose of new ideas can do a lot to boost your morale, energy and effectiveness.

Some of the best magazines specifically for business women are available as membership benefits from the associations listed in Chapter 4. Since these association magazines are not available on the newsstand or by subscription, we have not included them in this list. Most of the associations will send you a free copy of their publications for review when you request membership information. Don't be shy about indicating that you are considering joining a particular organization and telling the person you speak with that one of your criteria will be the quality of the group's magazines and newsletters.

How to Proceed

Many of the magazines below are available in libraries or at newsstands. For subscription information call or write the publisher.

Entrepreneur
Entrepreneur Magazine
P.O. Box 50368
Boulder CO 80321-0368
(800) 421 2300

Entrepreneur provides information on starting and running a business for the established or novice entrepreneur. Each issue includes a special section about women business owners called *Entrepreneurial Woman*.

Home Office Computing
P.O. Box 51344
Boulder CO 80321-1344
(800) 288-7812

This magazine covers diverse issues of interest to home-based business owners, focusing on issues of software and hardware selection, but including many other topics such as time management, efficient home office setup and more.

INC.
Subscription Services Department
P.O. Box 51534
Boulder, CO 80321-1534
(800) 234-0999

INC. features business profiles, tips and in-depth articles on running a business. One issue annually profiles top women-owned businesses.

Ms.
Matilda Publishing Inc.
P.O. Box 57118
Boulder CO 80321
(212) 719-9800

This is an influential and opinionated news magazine for women that emphasizes political and late-breaking news.

Working Woman
P.O. Box 3274
Harlan IA 51593
(800) 234-9675

This contains in-depth articles, tips and resources for all working women, including the self-employed. One issue annually features successful women entrepreneurs.

3
Selling to the Government

You might think that selling to the government is only for big business, but it's not. The federal government purchases nearly $200 billion worth of goods and services—from pencils and janitorial services to new building construction—from U.S. businesses. That's a big market, and the federal government has special programs in place to help women business owners get a piece of it.

Every year the SBA's Office of Women's Business Ownership works with all departments in the federal government to set annual goals for purchasing from women-owned businesses and to identify women-owned businesses that can fulfill specific contracts. A special contract category for purchases of $25,000 or less, called *small business set-asides*, requires federal agencies to purchase goods and services from small businesses. Since many women-owned enterprises fall into the small business category, set-asides also help level the playing field for women business owners.

Procurement and *contracting* are the official terms used to describe the process of selling to the government, because purchasing agents *contract* with you to *procure* your company's goods or services. There are also purchasing agents in state, county and municipal governments and private companies.

Included in this chapter is information about federal, state and private resources to help you get started. We have included only brief references to sponsoring agencies so that you don't get bogged down in unnecessary details. For more information about the federal agencies involved, see *A Guide to Federal Agencies*, on page viii. A review of the definitions of common terms on page 127 may also be helpful to you as you read this chapter.

Listings with a symbol like the ones bordering the bottom of this page describe programs or resources that are specifically for women.

Selling to the Federal Government

Get Started at the Small Business Administration

- **Publications and women's representatives get you started on the right track**
- **Sponsored by: The SBA's Office of Women's Business Ownership**

The Office of Women's Business Ownership (OWBO) can provide you with a wealth of information about procurement and a copy of the SBA publication *Women Business Owners: Selling to the Federal Government.* In addition to information about procurement procedures, this publication includes lists of contracting specialists across the country who can help you sell to federal offices in your area. Your OWBO representatives can also provide guidance on procurement issues, directing you to appropriate federal agencies and purchasing agents that might be interested in your company's products or services.

OWBO representatives also coordinate specialized training seminars for women business owners on how to sell to the federal government.

How to Proceed

To order a copy of *Women Business Owners: Selling to the Federal Government*, contact OWBO at the number below, or order a copy from the Government Printing Office (see page 50 for ordering information).

Small Business Administration
Office of Women's Business Ownership
409 Third St. SW, Sixth Floor
Washington DC 20416
(202) 205-6673

For information about upcoming specialized training seminars and for guidance in locating appropriate purchasing agents, contact your regional OWBO representative (see page 71).

Register with the Procurement Automated Source System (PASS)

- **A special database of small businesses keeps you in the running for contracting dollars**
- **Sponsored by: The SBA**

The PASS system, a computerized directory of small businesses interested in bidding on federal contracts, was set up to help small businesses get a fair share of federal procurement dollars. When you register, a profile of your company will be included in the directory. Federal purchasing agents and prime contractors will see your profile when they use the system to identify companies capable of bidding for particular contracts. Registration on PASS is free to small businesses. Purchasing agents and prime contractors are charged an access fee to use the system to identify companies capable of bidding on particular contracts.

How to Proceed

To register with PASS you must fill out a one-page self-mailer application form available from your regional SBA office or by writing to:

Small Business Administration
PASS Program
Mail Code 6256
409 Third St. SW
Washington DC 20416

Office of Procurement

- **SBA publications provide practical information and answers to common questions**
- **Sponsored by: The SBA**

The SBA Office of Procurement has two free publications that you shouldn't miss: *Procurement Assistance: A Practical Guide for Businesses Seeking Federal Contracts* and *The 25 Most-Asked Questions About Federal Procurement*. (This office is not set up to serve the public directly, but they will provide these excellent publications and help you in locating resources if other offices have not been able to answer your questions.)

How to Proceed

Call the office at (202) 205-7321 to request copies.

Office of Small and Disadvantaged Business Utilization

- **Special offices to help women business owners sell to the federal government**
- **Sponsored by: The federal government**

If you want to turn the federal government into a customer, the Office of Small and Disadvantaged Business Utilization (OSDBU) is a resource you won't want to miss. An OSDBU office has been set up in every major department in the federal government (like the Department of Agriculture and the Department of Defense) to help minorities, women and small business owners gain access to the federal procurement process.

You can contact the small business specialist or the women's business specialist in each department's OSDBU to determine if your products or services can fulfill any of their procurement requirements. Once you identify which agencies you might do business with, ask for the appropriate forms for being included on their solicitation mailing lists. Also request a list of each agencies' procurement offices and purchasing agents so you can begin marketing to them.

Two federal departments, the Department of Transportation and NASA, set aside specific dollar amounts annually which are earmarked for women-owned businesses. Those would be good doors to knock on first.

To give you an idea of what sort of assistance is available, we've profiled the Department of Commerce, which runs an active women's program.

U.S. Department of Commerce

The Department of Commerce's Office of Small and Disadvantaged Business Utilization is responsible for ensuring that small, minority and women-owned businesses receive a fair share of all federal contracts. As a part of that effort, the department increased its purchases from women-owned enterprises from $2.8 million dollars in 1980 to over $20 million in 1989.

Through its women's program, the department sponsors conferences and publishes directories, handbooks and bibliographies specifically for women business owners. In addition, women are actively sought to serve on the department's advisory boards and in technical programs.

Each year the Commerce Department's 14 bureaus, agencies and offices purchase everything from direct mail advertising services to X-ray equipment. Through its OSDBU office, staffed with a women's business specialist, the department offers personal counseling to women interested in selling to the federal government and to the Department of Commerce specifically.

The free publication *How to Sell to the United States Department of Commerce* is a good introduction to this market. It includes step-by-step information about how to get in the department's procurement pipeline, who to contact for different types of information and lists of what each bureau in the department purchases. (By checking this list, you will be able to determine pretty quickly if you can provide a service or product that Commerce needs.)

How to Proceed

For more information about selling to the U.S. Department of Commerce and to receive a copy of *How to Sell to the United States Department of Commerce*, contact the women's business specialist at:

The U.S. Department of Commerce
Office of Small and Disadvantaged Business Utilization (OSDBU)
14th & Constitution Ave.
Room H6411
Washington DC 20230
(202) 482-1472

For information about selling to other federal agencies, contact the OSDBU in each federal agency or department and ask for the small business specialist or women's business specialist or representative. (For a list of OSDBUs in all major federal agencies, see page 97.)

Certification Program for Women Business Owners

- **Become eligible for procurement dollars that are earmarked for women-owned businesses**
- **Sponsored by: State Departments of Transportation**

Odd as it may seem, your State Department of Transportation is a good office to contact for Women's Business Enterprise (WBE) certification. WBE certification takes place at the state level because a special program through the Federal Department of Transportation (DOT) sets aside contracting dollars earmarked for women-owned businesses. Each year, the federal DOT works with the state transportation departments to set goals for awarding construction contracts to individual states' women-owned businesses.

As a part of this process, the state transportation departments have begun certifying businesses that are owned 51% or more by women.

How to Proceed

See page 102 for a state-by-state listing of transportation departments. Also check the listing of first-stop state offices on page 91. Many of them are also involved in WBE certification.

Registration on the Automated Business Enterprise Locator System

- **An electronic database lets purchasing agents know about your business**
- **Sponsored by: The U.S. Department of Commerce Minority Business Development Agency**

The Automated Business Enterprise Locator System (ABELS) is an online computer directory set up to help purchasing agents in private businesses, state or municipal governments and the federal government identify minority businesses that can meet their needs for goods and services. ABELS is a free service to minority businesses and to the companies or government agencies which use the database.

How to Proceed

To register with ABELS, you need to fill out an ABELS Registration/Certification Form and return it to the U.S. Department of Commerce MBDA office listed below. Registration forms are available from your regional MBDA (see page 87) or from:

U.S. Department of Commerce
Minority Business Development Agency
Information Technology Branch
Room H5714
14th & Constitution Ave. NW
Washington DC 20230
(202) 482-1958

Commerce Business Daily: News on Selling Opportunities

■ **Commerce Department publication keeps you current on procurement opportunities**

Commerce Business Daily (CBD), published by the Department of Commerce, is a comprehensive source of information about upcoming opportunities to sell to the government. Included in each listing is the name and address of the agency looking for contractors, the service or product desired, the proposal deadline and phone number to request contract specifications information.

CBD also includes information about contract awards to companies that have recently received large government contracts. These large contractors, referred to as prime contractors, subcontract a portion of their work out, making opportunities available to smaller companies.

An annual subscription to CBD is approximately $270. Depending on your company's procurement potential, a subscription may or may not be a good investment. The state Procurement Technical Assistance Centers (see page 52) subscribe to the CBD and can make it available to you. Many large public libraries also subscribe. Check the section under private resources in this chapter also. CBD information targeted to your company's needs may be available at a more reasonable cost from private information brokers (page 54).

How to Proceed

To subscribe or to get an information booklet about CBD, contact the Superintendent of Documents Order and Information Desk at (202) 783-3238 or write to:

Superintendent of Documents
U.S. Government Printing Office
Washington DC 20402

Government Printing Office Procurement Publications

■ **Low-cost guides to the world of government contracting**

In addition to the publication *Women Business Owners: Selling to the Federal Government* described earlier, many other useful government publications on procurement are available. *Doing Business with the Federal Government* is a good place to start to get a general overview. Combined with more specialized books on a variety of topics (selling to the military, for instance), these publications can be an inexpensive way to educate yourself on how to succeed in the government contracting arena.

How to Proceed

To get more information about procurement booklets, call or visit a government bookstore in your area (see page 116). To receive a brochure of publications about selling to the government, contact:

Superintendent of Documents
U.S. Government Printing Office
Mail Stop SM
Room 3123
Washington DC 20402
(202) 783-3238

More Tips on How to Get Started

The information here is just the first of many things you will need to do to get your foot in the door. Find out as much as you can about government purchasing needs by talking to procurement specialists and purchasing agents, reading each department's guidelines and by attending training sessions on selling to the government. Also, there will be many regional and departmental procurement specialists listed in publications you receive from the SBA, the U.S. Department of Commerce and other offices. Contact those that are appropriate, either because they work specifically in your geographic area or because you can fulfill their needs.

The most important thing, though, is to make yourself known to the purchasing agents. Contact them personally if you have determined you have something they need, send your product or service information to them, attend procurement fairs where you will meet purchasing agents and register on PASS (see page 46) and, if you are a minority business owner, ABELS (see page 49).

Selling to State Governments

Certification Program for Woman Business Owners

- Become eligible for state, local and private procurement dollars that are set aside for women-owned businesses
- Sponsored by: State Departments of Transportation

In the previous section, *Selling to the Federal Government*, we described why WBE certification occurs on the state level and is usually handled by state transportation departments (page 49).

WBE certification can help you get contracts from state, county and local agencies (as well as from private companies) that are interested in purchasing services and products from women-owned businesses. Many transportation departments also publish a state directory of WBE-certified businesses, which is used by purchasing agents to identify vendor businesses.

In addition to contacting your state transportation department about WBE certification, you should also consider contacting them if you can provide goods or services needed in highway construction and maintenance.

How to Proceed

See page 102 for a state-by-state listing of transportation departments. Also check the list of first-stop state offices on page 91. Many of them are also involved in WBE certification.

Procurement Technical Assistance Centers

- Agencies across the country provide contracting assistance close to home
- Sponsored by: State and federal governments

If you want to get in on selling to state and municipal agencies in your area as well as to federal offices, there is help right in your backyard. Almost every state has at least one Procurement Technical Assistance Center to help educate business owners about contracting opportunities at the federal, state and local level.

The programs and services offered vary by state, but to give you an idea of what resources you might find, we have included a description of the program in our home state of Oregon, where there are five assistance center offices.

PROFILE

Oregon's Procurement Assistance Program

The Oregon program is comprehensive, helping businesses find contracting opportunities, meet bidding and agency requirements, prepare proposals and even collect payment for completed work. The offices offer workshops, seminars and individual training in all aspects of the procurement process.

Oregon has developed its own procurement database and electronic bulletin board. Procurement specialists use this database in conjunction with the *Commerce Business Daily* and other resources to hook clients up with the right opportunities. Clients can also get information from the system by logging on with a computer and modem.

In Oregon, there has been a strong effort to help businesses sell to their state, county and local government agencies. The packet of material we received, which included registration forms and an overview of the program, also had lists of purchasing agents in state, county and municipal offices.

How to Proceed

Contact the office closest to you in your state. (See page 107 for a state-by-state listing of assistance centers.) In reviewing the list, you will see that some offices specialize in certain areas, such as Indian affairs or defense purchasing. If there is more than one office in your area, select one that is appropriate for your interests.

Private Sources of Procurement Information

Electronic Information Brokers Give You the Edge

Information about opportunities to sell to federal agencies, including news from *Commerce Business Daily*, is available in electronic and printed form from a number of private companies. Information about state and local government contracts is also available from some of the services. The information provided—and the procedures for obtaining it—vary from company to company, so check with each one.

Some companies can look for contract opportunities in the private and public sector that specifically request proposals from women-owned businesses. To give you an idea of how these services work, we have profiled one company below.

Softshare Government Information Services

Softshare makes information available in electronic or printed form to subscribers. An interactive online system is available 24 hours a day, as well as an electronic system which keeps you informed of contract opportunities that match key search terms you have selected (like women-owned and/or office supplies, etc.). Softshare staff members are available to help you design an effective search strategy. The Softsearch database includes information on federal, state, local and foreign market opportunities.

In addition to search services, Softshare offers a reporting system, called SMART, that provides market information about your industry's activity in federal contracting. With SMART, you can find out who is buying how much from what companies and base your marketing strategy on that information.

In cases in which an agency accepts electronic submission of proposals, Softshare can help you submit them properly, ensuring that your response is received before bid deadlines.

How to Proceed

Request information from the companies below and select the one most appropriate for your needs.

Alden Electronics
40 Washington St.
Westboro MA 01581
(800) 876-1232

CBD Fax Service
48 Harbor Park Dr.
90 Merrick Ave.
Port Washington NY 11050
(516) 626-2090

CBD OnLine
11300 Rockville Pike Station
Suite 1100
Rockville MD 20852
(301) 816-8950 Ext. 400

CBD Search Services
21525 Ridgetop Circle
Suite 200
Sterling VA 20166
(800) 223-4551

Dialog Information Services
3460 Hillview Ave.
Palo Alto CA 94304
(800) 334-2564

Government Access and Information Network (GAIN)

(For more information about this interactive fax service, see page 30.)

Mead Data Central
P.O. Box 933
Dayton OH 45401
(800) 543-6862

Mercury Electronic Publishing (MEPCO)
222 S. Market St.
Suite 104
Elizabethtown PA 17022
(800) 669-2441

Sales Opportunity Services
1538 Rear East Pleasant Valley Blvd.
Altoona PA 16602
(800) 225-6853

Softshare Government Information Services
2241 Stanwood Dr.
Santa Barbara CA 93103
(800) 346-6703

National Minority Business Council (NMBC)

■ **Ongoing assistance and resources for an annual membership fee**

NMBC provides training and procurement assistance to minority-owned businesses. Women are not specifically included in the organization's primary definition of *minority*, but all women-owned minority businesses are eligible for membership.

Membership benefits include international trade assistance, referral of your business to buying agents through a computerized directory, a free listing in the *Corporate Purchasing Directory*, a subscription to the bimonthly newsletter *NMBC Business Report* and discounts on business travel services.

How to Proceed:

Call or write the council at:

National Minority Business Council (NMBC)
235 E. 42nd St.
New York NY 10017
(212) 573-2385

4

Membership Organizations

This chapter includes names, addresses and phone numbers for three types of national organizations:

- Women's business organizations
- Women's professional organizations
- General business associations

By identifying and joining those organizations that match your interests, you can tap into a large network of other like-minded businesswomen, receive regular association magazines and newsletters and take advantage of educational and professional development opportunities on a national and regional level.

When contacting those that sound interesting, ask for samples of their publications and past conference flyers so you can determine if the organization's activities and focus match your needs. Some associations offer subscriptions and conference attendance to non-members, so ask about these options also if you like some aspects of the organization but don't want to make a membership commitment.

Women's Business Associations

The organizations included in this section operate specifically to meet the needs of women business owners and entrepreneurs. Each organization has a different focus, designed to meet the needs and interests of particular segments within the women's business ownership community.

Alliance of Minority Women for Business and Political Development
909 Pershing Dr.
Suite 200
Silver Springs MD 20910
(301) 565-0258

This organization encourages networking, joint ventures, information exchange and political action among its members. Minority women business owners in a wide range of services and industries are eligible for membership.

American Business Women's Association (ABWA)
9100 Ward Parkway
P.O. Box 8728
Kansas City MO 64114-0728
(816) 361-6621

With a membership of over 100,000 businesswomen in the United States and Puerto Rico, ABWA brings together women of diverse backgrounds to provide professional and personal development opportunities. Membership benefits include *Women in Business* magazine, national and regional conferences, discounts on travel, prescriptions and other products, accidental death or dismemberment insurance and no-annual fee credit cards.

American Women in Enterprise (AWE)
71 Vanderbuilt Ave.
3rd Floor
New York NY 10169
(212) 688-1900

AWE membership benefits include access to a telephone hotline for up to 10 minutes of expert advice on an urgent issue, a subscription to the *Women in Enterprise* newsletter, networking events, an annual conference, and a variety of purchasing opportunities including access to a buying service for major purchases such as business equipment and cars. Membership also includes discounts on services from the American Women's Economic Development Corporation (AWED), an entrepreneurial training center that offers expert training and counseling in every phase of business growth, development and management. Program participants have access to courses and personal and telephone counseling.

Association of African-American Women Business Owners
P.O. Box 13933
Silver Springs MD 20911
(301) 565-0258

Geared to small business owners in all industries, particularly service businesses, the association provides networking opportunities, personal development programs and legislative action opportunities for its members.

Association of Black Women Entrepreneurs Inc. (ABWE)
P.O. Box 49368
Los Angeles CA 90049
(213) 624-8639

ABWE provides members with business and educational support through networking, referrals, joint ventures, mentoring opportunities, a quarterly newsletter, seminars and one call annually to consult on a business issue.

The Committee of 200
625 N. Michigan Ave.
Suite 500
Chicago IL 60611
(312) 751-3477

Members of The Committee of 200 are presidents, owners or high-level decision-makers of companies with revenues typically exceeding $10 million annually. The organization has established a foundation dedicated to recognizing and fostering entrepreneurship in women. Scholarships, outreach seminars and other activities are provided to women in business through the foundation.

The International Alliance (TIA)
8600 LaSalle Rd., Suite 617
Baltimore MD 21286
(410) 472-4221

The alliance serves as a central forum for women's networks across the country by providing members with leadership and skill training, promoting greater recognition of women's achievements and helping public and private organizations identify female expertise. The association sponsors an annual conference, network meetings and a speaker's bank, and publishes a bimonthly newsletter and membership directory.

National Association of Women Business Owners (NAWBO)
1377 K. St. NW
Suite 637
Washington DC 20005
(301) 608-2590

NAWBO, the official U.S. member of the World Association of Women Entrepreneurs, is the only national organization that represents all women business owners. Its membership benefits include national and international networking, management and technical assistance at the local chapter level, and newsletters. It also offers the opportunity to learn about and participate in international trade through trade missions and international conferences, and gives you access to a directory of women business owners in 23 countries.

Members also receive access to product and service discount purchasing. NAWBO founded the National Foundation for Women Business Owners, a non-profit organization which collects and reports data on women's business ownership issues and develops women's business training programs.

National Association of Minority Women in Business (NAMWIB)
906 Grand Ave.
Suite 200
Kansas City MO 64106
(816) 421-3335

Serving as a network for the exchange of ideas, information and business opportunities for business owners and management, the association offers workshops, conferences and seminars, compiles statistics, maintains a speaker's bureau and publishes a bi-monthly membership newsletter.

National Federation of Business and Professional Women's Clubs (BPW)
2012 Massachusetts Ave. NW
Washington DC 20036
(202) 293-1100

This is an advocacy and educational organization for working women, including business owners. The organization runs the BPW Foundation, a non-profit research and educational organization, and BPW Political Action Committee that provides contributions to and endorses women and pro-women candidates. Membership benefits include *National Business Woman* magazine, advocacy in Washington and assistance in developing advocacy programs, a legislative hotline, skill-building programs, annual conventions and access to loans, insurance purchase and other product and service discounts.

National Women's Economic Alliance Foundation (NWEAF)
1440 New York Ave. NW
Suite 300
Washington DC 20005
(202) 393-5257

This foundation addresses issues of professional, economic and career development of executive-level men and women in the free enterprise system. The organization conducts research, provides a placement service and offers leadership training. Members receive a semi-annual newsletter, periodic policy papers and an annual directory of new women entrepreneurs.

National Association for Women in Careers (NAWIC)
675 N. Court
Suite 200
Palatine IL 60067
(708) 358-4965

This association helps women address the issues of balancing career demands with private life by offering opportunities for personal and professional growth through workshops, newsletters, leadership training, and networking. New members receive a career kit.

National Association for Female Executives (NAFE)
30 Irving Place, 5th Floor
New York NY 10003
(212) 477-2200

NAFE, a networking and professional development organization, offers contacts and support across the country through its extensive network of local member groups. NAFE offers an array of member benefits, including satellite conferences, access to a loan and venture capital fund, career assistance and an excellent full-color magazine, *Executive Female*. NAFE also offers member benefit programs in the areas of financial services, discount purchasing, travel and car rental discounts, travel services, insurance and health benefits.

National Chamber of Commerce for Women
10 Waterside Plaza
Suite 6H
New York NY 10010
(212) 685-3454

The chamber makes a variety of resources and services available to working and self-employed women through participation on four committees that target members' needs. The committees include The Business Owner's Advisory, The Home-Based Committee, The Productivity Improvement Network and The World of Women's Business Committee. Assistance is provided through a combination of mentoring, phone counseling, access to information banks and attendance at free workshops. For more specific information about the committees and services, see page 15.

Wider Opportunity for Women (WOW)
1325 G St. NW
Lower Level
Washington DC 20005
(202) 638-3143

WOW works to achieve economic independence and equality of opportunity for women and girls, advocating for non-traditional work opportunities for women in every state and the District of Columbia. WOW leads the Women's Work Force Network of over 500 independent women's employment programs. A membership branch provides career development, training and other work-related assistance services.

Women in Franchising (WIF)
53 West Jackson St.
Suite 756
Chicago IL 60604
(800) 222-4943
(312) 431-1467

This organization serves as an information resource for women interested in franchising. To receive information from companies in your area of interest that are looking for women franchisees, you can send WIF $12 along with a completed questionnaire about your franchise interests, your business background, areas of expertise, your ability to purchase a franchise and your income goals. The $12 buys you a year's worth of information.

Women's Economic Round Table (WERT)
866 United Nations Plaza
Suite 4052
New York NY 10017
(212) 759-4360

This organization works to inform and educate its members and the public about important economic issues of our times and to encourage its members to actively influence policy makers. To further its mission, WERT sponsors public forums and member seminars, participates in media coverage of economic issues and serves as a resource center to business, government and academia.

Women's Professional Associations

The professional groups listed here provide a way for women in specific fields to network with their colleagues, attend seminars and conferences within their industry and receive publications of interest in specific fields of expertise.

American Society of Women Accountants (ASWA)
1755 Lynnfield Road
Suite 222
Memphis TN 38119-7235
(800) 326-2163
(901) 680-0470

ASWA offers members an array of professional development opportunities through annual and regional conferences, job referral, career counseling, leadership training, and mentoring. Members receive a monthly newsletter, a membership directory, product and service purchasing discounts (such as subscriptions and car rentals) and are eligible for the member loan program. Educational scholarships are also available to support women interested in entering the accounting field.

Association for Women in Computing (AWC)
41 Sutter St.
Suite 1006
San Francisco CA 94104
(415) 905-4663

This association works to advance the role of women in the computing industry and to keep its members informed about legal, technical and other issues related to computing. The association offers opportunities for professional development through technical training, motivational seminars, and networking. Members receive the association quarterly, *NewsBytes*.

Financial Women International (FWI)
7910 Woodmont Ave., Suite 1430
Bethesda MD 20814-3015
(301) 657-8288

FWI, the largest individual membership organization of women financial executives today, works to keep its members in touch with every facet of the financial industry and in step with local, national and global economic trends. Each member receives a free annual portfolio review which helps them assess their strengths and weaknesses and to set goals and explore ways to achieve them. The organization offers continuing education self-study courses and management and leadership training. Included in the cost of membership are subscriptions to the organization's publications *FWI Management Quarterly* and *Financial Women Today*.

National Association of Black Women Attorneys, Inc. (NABWA)
3711 Macomb St. NW
Washington DC 20016
(202) 966-9693

This association's primary missions are to address special problems of being a black women attorney and to help black female law students through a scholarship fund. Although NABWA is a professional organization, its membership is open to non-lawyers interested in helping advance the organization's purpose.

National Association of Women in Insurance (NAWI)
P.O. Box 4410
Tulsa OK 74159
(800) 766-6249
(918) 744-5195

A professional development and networking organization, NAWI's primary mission is to increase the number of women in leadership positions in the insurance industry through public relations efforts, leadership training and certification of individual members as Certified Professional Insurance Women. Membership benefits include subscriptions to *Today's Insurance Woman* and *Leadership News*, a toll-free answer line, educational publications and meetings and discount product and service purchasing.

National Association of Women in Construction (NAWIC)
327 South Adams St.
Fort Worth TX 76104
(800) 552-3506
(817) 877-5551

This group works to promote acceptance and advancement of women in the construction industry and educates members in new construction techniques. National and local scholarships are available for engineering construction or architecture students. Members receive the monthly association magazine.

National Association of Women Lawyers (NAWL)
American Bar Center
750 N. Lake Shore Drive
Chicago IL 60611
(312) 988-6186

Affiliated with the American Bar Association, the International Bar Association and the International Federation of Women Lawyers, NAWL works to advance the role of women in the legal profession and the judiciary. The association selects and endorses qualified lawyers for public office and all levels of the judiciary. It has a voting delegate in the House of Delegates of the American Bar Association and works through a variety of commissions and federations to improve the status of women in the profession and women in the legal system in general. Membership benefits include a mentorship program for recently admitted attorneys, educational opportunities at annual, regional meetings and a subscription to the *President's Newsletter* and a quarterly publication, *Women Lawyers Journal*.

Society of Women Engineers (SWE)
120 Wall St.
New York NY 10005
(212) 509-9577

The membership of this non-profit organization is made up of graduate engineers and men and women with equivalent engineering experience. The specific objectives of the society are: to inform young women, their parents, counselors, and the general public of the qualifications and achievements of women engineers and the opportunities open to them; to assist women engineers in readying themselves for a return to active work after temporary retirement; to serve as a center of information on women in engineering; and to encourage women engineers to attain high levels of education and professional achievement. The society sponsors an annual convention and student conference that includes technical sessions, workshops, tours and industrial exhibits.

Women in Agribusiness (WIA)
P.O. Box 10241
Kansas City MO 64111
(No telephone number available)

The organization's purpose is to organize women in agribusiness and to provide a forum on relevant issues in their field. Membership benefits include a newsletter, membership directory and networking opportunities.

Women in Aerospace (WIA)
922 Pennsylvania Ave. SE
Washington DC 20003
(202) 547-9451

The only professional organization that provides a formal network for women working in the aerospace field, WIA works to expand women's advancement opportunities in the field and to increase women's visibility as aerospace professionals. Membership benefits include a quarterly newsletter, membership directory, site visits and an annual conference.

Women in Communications, Inc. (WICI)
3717 Columbia Pike
Suite 310
Arlington VA 22204
(703) 920-5555

This organization offers educational and networking opportunities to professional communicators in print and broadcast journalism, public relations, marketing, advertising, publishing, technical writing, film and design as well as to educators in the communications field. Members receive the association magazine *The Professional Communicator*, access to a toll-free job hotline, a membership and resource directory, and a variety of publications, professional development kits and resource materials.

Women in Information Processing (WIP)
Lock Box 39173
Washington DC 20016
(202) 328-6161

WIP provides a forum for professionals in the computer, robotics and telecommunications fields and any related disciplines. Membership benefits include access to a speaker's bureau, monthly seminars, résumé guidance, a scholarship program and the organization's annual Salary and Perception Survey.

Women in Management (WIM)
30 North Michigan Ave.
Suite 508
Chicago IL 60602
(312) 263-3636

This organization provides professional development, networking, and educational opportunities for women in leadership and management roles. Membership benefits include a newsletter subscription, attendance at special presentations, management conferences and leadership training events.

Women Life Underwriters Confederation (WLUC)
17 South High St., Suite 1200
Columbus OH 43215
(800) 776-3008

Women in the insurance field are eligible for this group's membership benefits, including a mentorship program, accredited continuing education, leadership training, regional retreats, and educational conferences.

Women's Council of Realtors (WCR)
430 North Michigan Ave.
Chicago IL 60611-4093
(312) 329-8483

The only professional women's group of the National Association of Realtors, the council offers members opportunities for professional development through a four-part leadership training course, referral and relocation certification courses, educational conferences and a monthly magazine, *Communique*. Members also have access to discount buying services, a speaker's bureau, financial planning seminars and a national referral network.

General Business Associations

The membership organizations included here are not specifically for women, but offer excellent learning opportunities, access to business information and participation in discount buying services.

American Entrepreneurs Association (AEA)
2392 Morse Ave.
Irvine CA 92714
(714) 261-2325

Affiliated with *Entrepreneur* magazine, membership in this organization includes discounts on a subscription to *Entrepreneur*, business publications and software, seminars around the country. Discount buying services for travel, car rental and other types of services are also available. Members receive an association newsletter in addition to the magazine.

American Management Association (AMA)
135 West 50th St.
New York NY 10020
(212) 586-8100

The AMA offers a wide range of educational and professional development opportunities through attendance at conferences, enrollment in AMA courses on specialized management topics, and self-study courses. Members are eligible for reduced purchase and rental rates on a variety of books, publications and training videos and receive the association publications *Management Review* and *Forum*. Members have access to The Information Resource Center in New York City and free use of state-of-the-art meeting facilities in the New York, Chicago, Atlanta and Washington D.C. Management Centers. A special membership category for growing companies has been established to meet their special needs.

National Alliance of Business (NAB)
National Headquarters
1201 New York Ave. NW
Suite 700
Washington DC 20005-3917
(202) 289-2888

NAB works toward development of national strategies and programs to improve the quality of the American work force by bringing together leaders in government, business, education and labor. It offers conferences, technical assistance services (such as on-site training and help in accessing public and private business resources) and publications and videos on work, management and training issues. Members receive Alliance publications *WorkAmerica* and *Business Currents*, as well as periodic technical reports. NAB has six service centers around the country. For more information about NAB and to be directed to the service center that serves your area, contact the national headquarters.

National Association for the Self Employed (NASE)
P.O. Box 612067
Dallas TX 75261-9968
(800) 232-6273

This association has a full-time staff dedicated to negotiating deals on high-value benefits such as financial services and health care, publications, travel savings and family-fun discounts. Members receive the NASE newspaper, *Self-Employed America*.

National Association for the Cottage Industry (NACI)
P.O. Box 14850
Chicago IL 60614
(312) 472-8116

This organization offers people who work from their homes access to information on business organizational methods, marketing and promotion, zoning, taxes, licensing requirements and other topics of interest.

National Association of Private Enterprise (NAPE)
P.O. Box 612147
Dallas TX 75261-2147
(800) 223-6273
(817) 428-4200

NAPE is the *small* small business owners association. Set up to serve businesses with 10 or fewer employees, the association represents small business in Washington D.C., provides free consulting on tax, legal, marketing and other issues, educational scholarships, medical insurance and discounts on a variety of business services and products, including long-distance service, office supplies and credit card processing.

National Business Association (NBA)
P.O. Box 870728
Dallas TX 75287
(800) 456-0440
(214) 991-5381

This association provides entrepreneurs and small business owners with an array of services and products to help them run their businesses more effectively and to enjoy their time away from work. It provides services and products for business management and financial planning, education, health and personal fitness, and lifestyle management. Products range from productivity software and health insurance to financial products or travel discounts. Members also receive the association newsletter, *National Business News*.

National Federation of Independent Businesses (NFIB)
53 Century Boulevard
Suite 3000
Nashville TN 37214
(615) 872-5312

Serving as the small business owner's political voice, the federation represents small business interests to state and federal legislators and other decision-making bodies through lobbying efforts and research. The organization's track record includes influencing passage of laws that simplified payroll tax deposit procedures and gave small businesses phase-in and tax credit options to meet new disability laws. Legislative positions of the organization are determined by a membership vote.

National Minority Business Council (NMBC)
235 E. 42nd St.
New York NY 10017
(212) 573-2385

The council provides training and procurement assistance to minority-owned businesses. Women are not specifically included in the organization's primary definition of *minority*, but all women-owned minority businesses are eligible for membership. Benefits include international trade assistance, referral of your business to buying agents through a computerized directory, free listing in the Corporate Purchasing Directory, a subscription to the bimonthly newsletter *NMBC Business Report* and discounts on business travel services.

Renaissance Business Associates (RBA)
P.O. Box 26510
Colorado Springs CO 80936-6510
(719) 495-9617

An international organization for business people committed to ethical, socially responsible business practices, this association sponsors an annual conference, local and regional seminars, a mentoring program and a speaker's bureau. Members receive a bimonthly newsletter, *Business Dynamics*.

The Leads Club
P.O. Box 279
Carlsbad CA 92018
(800) 783-3761
(619) 729-7797

The Leads Club is a networking organization that provides services and education through its national office, and business-building opportunities through local networking groups designed to generate business referrals and leads. Originally for women only, most chapters are now co-ed. Members receive a regular newsletter from headquarters that provides marketing tips, inspiration and success stories.

5

Resources, Programs and Agencies

The listings in this chapter are all referred to in other parts of this guide. As stand-alone lists, they will not be of much use, but the rest of this guide makes reference to every list included here. As you begin to get a feel for the kinds of help a particular agency can offer, you will be able to use the listings independently from the rest of the book.

The Quick-Find Guide on the next page is designed to help you locate the agency or office you are looking for without having to check back to the original reference in a previous chapter.

In general, we have not included individuals' names in the listings because they change so frequently. At the beginning of each list, we tell you who to ask for by title or what specific information to ask for when you contact an agency. This approach should get you routed to the right person. In two lists (SCORE Women's Coordinators and Women's Business Advocates) we have included the names of people you must contact individually for assistance.

Quick-Find Guide

SBA Regional Offices 69

SBA Women's Business Representatives
(Office of Women's Business Ownership) 71

Women's Business Development Centers (OWBO Demonstration Sites) . . . 77

Small Business Development Centers (SBDCs) 80

SCORE Women's Business Coordinators 85

Minority Business Development Agencies (MBDA) Regional Offices 87

Women's Bureau, U.S. Department of Labor (Regional Offices) 89

First-Stop State Offices 91

Office of Small and Disadvantaged Business Utilization (OSDBU) 97

State Departments of Transportation 102

Procurement Technical Assistance Centers 107

Federal Information Centers 115

U. S. Government Bookstores 116

State Women's Business Advocates 118

National Association of Women's Yellow Pages 125

SBA Regional Offices

There are 10 SBA regions, each one served by a head office and a number of field offices. Contact the office below that serves your state to find out about general SBA services in your area and to get directed to appropriate field offices and personnel. For more information about the SBA and its programs, review *A Guide to Federal Agencies* (page viii) and the sections on federal resources in Chapters 1 and 2 and 3.

Region 1

Maine, Vermont, Massachusetts, New Hampshire, Connecticut, Rhode Island

Small Business Administration
155 Federal St., 9th Floor
Boston MA 02110
(617) 451-2030 TDD: (617) 451-1491

Region 2

New York, New Jersey, Puerto Rico, Virgin Islands

Small Business Administration
26 Federal Plaza, Room 31-08
New York NY 10278
(212) 264-1450 TDD: (212) 264-5669

Region 3

Pennsylvania, Delaware, Maryland, Virginia, Washington D.C., West Virginia

Small Business Administration
475 Allendale Road, Suite 201
King of Prussia PA 19406
(215) 962-3700 TDD: (215) 962-3739

Region 4

North Carolina, South Carolina, Kentucky, Tennessee, Georgia, Alabama, Mississippi, Florida

Small Business Administration
1375 Peachtree St. NE, 5th Floor
Atlanta GA 30367-8102
(404) 347-2797 TDD: (404) 347-5051

Region 5

Minnesota, Wisconsin, Michigan, Ohio, Indiana, Illinois

Small Business Administration
300 S. Riverside Plaza, Suite 1975 S
Chicago IL 60606-6617
(312) 353-5000 TDD: (312) 353-8060

Region 6

New Mexico, Texas, Oklahoma, Arkansas, Louisiana

Small Business Administration
8625 King George Drive, Bldg. C
Dallas TX 75235-3391
(214) 767-7633   TDD: (214) 767-1339

Region 7

Kansas, Missouri, Iowa, Nebraska

Small Business Administration
911 Walnut St., 13th Floor
Kansas City MO 64106
(816) 426-3608   TDD: (816) 426-2990

Region 8

Montana, North Dakota, South Dakota, Wyoming, Utah, Colorado

Small Business Administration
999 18th St., Suite 701
Denver CO 80202
(303) 294-7186   TDD: (303) 294-7096

Region 9

California, Nevada, Arizona, Hawaii

Small Business Administration
71 Stevenson St., 20th Floor
San Francisco CA 94105-2939
(415) 744-6402   TDD: (415) 744-6401

Region 10

Washington, Oregon, Idaho, Alaska

Small Business Administration
2615 4th Ave., Room 440
Seattle WA 98121
(206) 553-5676   TDD: (206) 553-2872

SBA Women's Representatives
(Office of Women's Business Ownership)

Each of the offices below has a women's business representative on staff. Contact the closest representative in your region for information about women's business ownership programs in your area. For more information about the Office of Women's Business Ownership and its programs, review *A Guide to the Federal Agencies* (page viii) in the introduction and the beginning of the section on federal resources in Chapters 1 and 2.

Region 1

**Maine, Vermont, Massachusetts,
New Hampshire, Connecticut, Rhode Island**

Small Business Administration
155 Federal St., 9th Floor
Boston MA 02110
(617) 451-2023

Small Business Administration
330 Main St., 2nd Floor
Hartford CT 06106
(203) 240-4642

Small Business Administration
10 Causeway St., Room 265
Boston MA 02222-1093
(617) 565-5588

Small Business Administration
87 State St., Room 205
P.O. Box 605
Montpelier VT 05601
(802) 828-4422

Small Business Administration
40 Western Ave., Room 512
Augusta ME 04330
(207) 622-8242

Small Business Administration
380 Westminister Mall
Providence RI 02903
(401) 528-4598

Small Business Administration
Stewart Nelson Plaza, 2nd Floor
143 N. Main St., P.O. Box 1257
Concord NH 03302-1257
(603) 225-1400

Small Business Administration
1550 Main St., Room 212
Springfield MA 01103
(413) 785-0268

Region 2

**New York, New Jersey,
Puerto Rico, Virgin Islands**

Small Business Administration
26 Federal Plaza, Room 3100
New York NY 10278
(212) 264-1468

Small Business Administration
100 S. Clinton St., Room 1071
Syracuse NY 13260
(315) 423-5375

Small Business Administration
Elmira Savings Bank Building
333 East Water St.
Elmira NY 14901
(607) 734-8142

Small Business Administration
Military Park Building
60 Park Place, 4th Floor
Newark NJ 07102
(201) 645-3683

Small Business Administration
111 W. Huron St., Room 1311
Buffalo NY 14202
(716) 846-4517

Small Business Administration
Carlos Chardon Ave.
Hato Rey PR 00918
(809) 766-5001

Small Business Administration
35 Pinelawn Road, Room 102E
Melville NY 11747
(516) 454-0753

Small Business Administration
Leo O'Brien Building, Room 815
Clinton and Pearl Sts.
Albany NY 12207
(518) 472-4300

Small Business Administration
United Shopping Plaza, Room 7
4 C/D State Sion Farm
Christiansted
St. Croix, Virgin Islands 00801
(809) 778-5380

Small Business Administration
Federal Office Building, Room 283
Veterans Drive
St. Thomas, Virgin Islands 00801
(809) 774-8530

Small Business Administration
Federal Building
100 State St.
Rochester NY 14614
(716) 263-6700

Region 3

Pennsylvania, Delaware, Maryland, Virginia, Washington D.C., W. Virginia

Small Business Administration
475 Allendale Road
Suite 201
King of Prussia PA 19406
(215) 962-3818

Small Business Administration
960 Penn Ave., 5th Floor
Pittsburgh PA 15222
(412) 644-2785

Small Business Administration
400 North 8th St., Room 3015
P.O. Box 10126
Richmond VA 23240
(804) 771-2765 Ext. 112

Small Business Administration
10 North Calvert St., 4th Floor
Baltimore MD 21202
(401) 962-6149 Ext. 338

Small Business Administration
1110 Vermont Ave. NW, Suite 900
Washington DC 20043
(202) 606-4000 Ext. 258

Small Business Administration
168 West Main St.
P.O. Box 1608
Clarksburg WV 26302
(304) 623-5631

Small Business Administration
One Rodney Square, Suite 412
920 North King St.
Wilmington DE 19801
(302) 573-6295

Region 4

North Carolina, South Carolina, Kentucky, Tennessee, Georgia, Alabama, Mississippi, Florida

Small Business Administration
1375 Peachtree St. NE
Atlanta GA 30367
(404) 347-2245

Small Business Administration
1 Hancock Plaza, Suite 1001
Gulfport MS 39501
(601) 863-4449

Small Business Administration
1720 Peachtree St., NW, 6th Fl
Atlanta GA 30309
(404) 347-2356

Small Business Administration
7825 Bay Meadows Way
Suite 100B
Jacksonville FL 32256-7504
(904) 443-1912

Small Business Administration
2121 8th Ave., Suite 200
Birmingham AL 35203-2398
(205) 731-1338

Small Business Administration
600 Dr. MLK, Jr. Place
Room 188
Louisville KY 40201
(502) 582-5971

Small Business Administration
200 North College St., Suite A2015
Charlotte NC 28202-2173
(704) 344-6587

Small Business Administration
1320 S. Dixie Hwy., Suite 501
Miami FL 33146
(305) 536-5521

Small Business Administration
50 Vantage Way, Suite 201
Nashville TN 37228
(615) 736-7176

Small Business Administration
1835 Assembly St., Room 358
Columbia SC 29202
(803) 253-3360

Small Business Administration
101 West Capitol St., Suite 400
Jackson MS 39201
(601) 965-5323

Region 5

Minnesota, Wisconsin, Michigan, Ohio, Indiana, Illinois

Small Business Administration
300 South Riverside Plaza
Suite 1975 South
Chicago IL 60606
(312) 353-5000 Ext. 764

Small Business Administration
500 West Madison St., Suite 1250
Chicago IL 60606
(312) 353-5429 Ext. 6243

Small Business Administration
212 E. Washington Ave., Rm. 213
Madison WI 53703
(608) 264-5516

Small Business Administration
Two Nationwide Plaza, Suite 1400
Columbus OH 43215-2542
(614) 469-6860 Ext. 274

Small Business Administration
525 Vine St., Room 870
Cincinnati OH 45202
(513) 684-6907

Small Business Administration
477 Michigan Ave.
Detroit, MI 48226
(313) 226-6075 Ext. 23

Small Business Administration
310 West Wisconsin Ave.
Milwaukee WI 53202
(414) 297-3941

Small Business Administration
429 North Pennsylvania St.
Suite 100
Indianapolis IN 46204
(317) 226-7272

Small Business Administration
511 West Capitol St.
Suite 302
Springfield IL 62704
(217) 492-4416

Small Business Administration
610 C Butler Square
Minneapolis MN 55403
(612) 370-2312

Small Business Administration
1111 Superior Ave., Suite 630
Cleveland OH 44114-2507
(216) 522-4180 Ext. 128

Region 6

New Mexico, Texas, Oklahoma, Arkansas, Louisiana

Small Business Administration
8625 King George Drive, Bldg. C
Dallas TX 75235-3391
(214) 767-7858

Small Business Administration
2120 Riverfront, Suite 100
Little Rock AR 72202
(501) 324-5871

Small Business Administration
222 E. Van Buren St., Suite 500
Harlingen TX 78550
(512) 427-8533

Small Business Administration
625 Silver SW, Room 320
Albuquerque NM 87102
(505) 766-1879

Small Business Administration
1611 10th St., Suite 200
Lubbock TX 79401
(806) 743-7462

Small Business Administration
9301 SW Freeway, Suite 550
Houston TX 77074
(713) 773-6549

Small Business Administration
1661 Canal St., 2nd Floor
New Orleans LA 70112
(504) 589-2354

Small Business Administration
200 NW 5th St., Suite 670
Federal Building
Oklahoma City OK 73102
(405) 231-4494

Small Business Administration
7400 Blanco Road, Suite 200
North Star Executive Center
San Antonio TX 78216
(210) 229-4535

Small Business Administration
10737 Gateway West, Suite 320
El Paso TX 79902
(915) 540-5564

Small Business Administration
606 N. Caranchua
Corpus Christi TX 78476
(512) 888-3301

Region 7

Kansas, Missouri, Iowa, Nebraska

Small Business Administration
911 Walnut St., 13th Floor
Kansas City MO 64106
(816) 426-5311

Small Business Administration
323 West 8th, 5th Floor
Kansas City MO 64106
(816) 374-6762

Small Business Administration
100 East English, Suite 510
Wichita KS 67202
(316) 269-6273

Small Business Administration
210 Walnut St., Room 749
Des Moines IA 50309
(515) 284-4761

Small Business Administration
11145 Mill Valley Road
Omaha NE 68154
(402) 221-3604

Small Business Administration
815 Olive St., Suite 242
St. Louis MO 63101
(314) 539-6600

Small Business Administration
373 Collins Road NE
Cedar Rapids IA 52402
(319) 393-8630

Small Business Administration
620 South Glenstone, Suite 110
Springfield MO 65802-3200
(417) 864-7670

Region 8

Montana, North Dakota, South Dakota, Wyoming, Utah, Colorado

Small Business Administration
999 18th St., Suite 701
Denver CO 80202
(303) 294-7067

Small Business Administration
721 19th St.
Denver CO 80202
(303) 844-3984

Small Business Administration
301 S. Park Ave., Room 528
Helena MT 59626-0054
(406) 449-5381

Small Business Administration
100 East B St., Room 4001
P.O. Box 2839
Casper WY 82602
(307) 261-5761

Small Business Administration
Federal Building
125 South State St.
Salt Lake City UT 84138-1195
(801) 524-6831

Small Business Administration
657 2nd Ave. North, Room 218
P.O. Box 3088
Fargo ND 58102
(701) 239-5131

Small Business Administration
101 S. Phillips Ave., Suite 200
Sioux Falls SD 57102
(605) 330-4231

Region 9

California, Nevada, Arizona, Hawaii

Small Business Administration
71 Stevenson St.
20th Floor
San Francisco CA 94105-2939
(415) 744-8491

Small Business Administration
330 N. Brand Blvd., Suite 1200
Glendale CA 91203-2304
(213) 894-4894

Small Business Administration
2719 N. Air Fresno Drive, Suite 107
Fresno CA 93727-1547
(209) 487-5605, Ext. 445

Small Business Administration
211 Main St., 4th Floor
San Francisco CA 94105-1988
(415) 744-8490

Small Business Administration
2828 N. Center Ave., Suite 800
Phoenix AZ 85004-1025
(602) 640-2316

Small Business Administration
30 Ala Moana, Room 2213
P.O. Box 50207
Honolulu HI 96850-4981
(808) 541-2974

Small Business Administration
800 Front St., Room 4-S-29
San Diego CA 92188-0270
(619) 557-7250 Ext. 1147

Small Business Administration
301 East Stewart, Box 7527
Downtown Station
Las Vegas NV 89125-2527
(702) 388-6611

Small Business Administration
901 W. Civic Center Drive, Suite 160
Santa Ana CA 92703-2352
(714) 836-2494 Ext. 3101

Small Business Administration
660 J St., Suite 215
Sacramento CA 95814-2413
(916) 551-1426

Region 10

Washington, Oregon, Idaho, Alaska

Small Business Administration
2615 4th St., Room 440
Seattle WA 98121-1233
(206) 553-8547

Small Business Administration
222 SW Columbia Ave., Room 500
Portland OR 97201-6605
(503) 326-5202

Small Business Administration
915 2nd Ave., Room 1792
Seattle WA 98174-1088
(206) 220-6523

Small Business Administration
West 601 First Ave.
10th Floor East
Spokane WA 99204-0317
(509) 353-2815

Small Business Administration
Federal Building, #67
222 West 8th Ave.
Anchorage AK 99513
(907) 271-4022

Small Business Administration
1020 Main St., Suite 290
Boise ID 83720
(208) 334-9079

Women's Business Development Centers (OWBO Demonstration Sites)

Check the listing for your state to see if there is a training site in your area. For more information about these programs, see page 2.

Alabama

Women's Yellow Pages of Greater Mobile, Inc.
1420 Government St.
P.O. Box 6021
Mobile AL 36660
(205) 473-5320

California

American Women's Economic Development Corp.
301 E. Ocean Blvd., Suite 1010
Long Beach CA 90802
(310) 983-3747

Women's Initiative for Self Employment
450 Mission St., Suite 402
San Francisco CA 94102
(415) 247-9473

WEST Co.
Women's Economic Self-Sufficiency
Training Program
340 N. Main St.
Fort Bragg CA 95437
(707) 964-7571

Colorado

Mi Casa Business Center for Women
571 Galapago St.
Denver CO 80204
(303) 573-1302

Connecticut

American Women's Economic Development Corporation (AWED)
2001 West Main St., Suite 140
Stamford CT 06902
(203) 326-7914

Georgia

Coalition of 100 Black Women
The Candler Building
127 Peachtree St. NE, Suite 700
Atlanta GA 30303
(404) 659-4008

Illinois

Women's Economic Venture Enterprise
229 16th St.
Rock Island IL 61201
(309) 788-9793
Serves Moline and Rock Island

Women's Business Development Center
8 South Michigan Ave., Suite 400
Chicago IL 60603
(312) 853-3477

Women's Business Development Center
SBDC/Joliet Junior College
214 N. Ottawa, 3rd Floor
Joliet IL 60431
(815) 727-6544 Ext. 1312

Women's Business Development Center
Kanakee Community College
4 Dearborn Square
Kanakee IL 60901
(815) 933-0375 FAX (815) 933-0380

Women's Business Owner's Advocacy Program
SBDC/Rock Valley College
1220 Rock St.
Rockford IL 61101
(815) 968-4087

Iowa

Women's Economic Venture Enterprise
229 16th St.
Rock Island IL 61201
(309) 788-9793
Serves Davenport and Bettendorf

Kentucky

Kentucky Mainstream Alliance
2909A Affirmed Court
Lexington KY 40509
(606) 257-4231

Michigan

EXCEL!
Midwest Women Business Owners
Development Team
200 Renaissance Center, Suite 1600
Detroit MI 48243-1274
(313) 396-3576 FAX (313) 396-3618

EXCEL!
Midwest Women Business Owners
Development Team
200 Ottawa NW, Suite 900
Grand Rapids MI 49503-2465
(616) 458-4783

Missouri

NAWBO of St. Louis
222 S. Bemiston, Suite 216
St. Louis MO 63105
(314) 863-0046

Minnesota

Bi-CAP, Inc.
Women in New Development
BI-CAP
P.O. Box 579
Bemidji MN 56601
(218) 751-4631

White Earth Reservation Tribal Council
P.O. Box 418
White Earth MN 56591
(218) 983-3285

Montana

Women's Opportunity and Resource Development Inc.
127 N. Higgins
Missoula MT 59802
(406) 543-3550

North Dakota

Maldan Management Company, Inc.
901 Page Drive
P.O. Box 9064
Fargo ND 68106-9064
(701) 235-6488

New Jersey

New Jersey NAWBO EXCEL
120 Finderne Ave.
P.O. Box 6336
Bridgewater NJ 08807
(908) 707-0173

New Mexico

Women's Economic Self-Sufficiency Team
414 Silver Southwest
Albuquerque NM 87102
(505) 848-4760

WESST Corp.
Taos County Economic Development Corporation
P.O. Box 1389
Taos NM 87571
(5050) 758-3099 FAX (505) 758-8153

New York

American Women's Economic Development Corporation
71 Vanderbilt Ave., Suite 320
New York NY 10169
(212) 688-1900

Ohio

Ohio Women's Business Resource Network
77 South High St., 28th Floor
Columbus OH 43266
(614) 593-1797

Cleveland Women's Business Development Center
City Hall, Room 335
601 Lakeside Ave.
Cleveland OH 44114
(216) 664-4159 or (216) 664-4162

Columbus Area Chamber of Commerce
37 North High St.
Columbus OH 43215-3065
(614) 225-6088 or (614) 221-1321

Women's Economic Assistance Ventures
100 Corry St.
P.O. Box 512
Yellow Springs OH 45387
(513) 767-2667

Women's Entrepreneurial Growth Organization
58 W. Center St.
P.O. Box 544
Akron OH 44309
(216) 535-9346

SBDC of Southeastern Ohio
One President St.
Athens OH 45701
(614) 593-1797 FAX (614) 593-1795

Women Entrepreneurs, Inc.
525 Vine St., 3rd Floor
Cincinnati OH 45202
(513) 684-0700

Pennsylvania

National Association of Women Business Owners
312 Boulevard of the Allies
Pittsburgh PA 15222
(412) 261-1235

Texas

Center for Women's Business Enterprise
2425 West Loop South, Suite 1004
Houston TX 77027
(713) 578-7061 Voicemail (713) 650-3833

Center for Women's Business Enterprise
2020 E. St. Elmo, Suite 130
Austin TX 78744
(512) 462-9705 FAX (512) 462-9470

Center for Women's Business Enterprise
2734 West Kingsley Rd., Suite 54
Garland TX 75041
(214) 278-1537

Southwest Resource Development
8700 Crownhill, Suite 700
San Antonio TX 78209
(210) 828-9034 (210) 828-4748

Washington D.C.

American Woman's Economic Development Corporation (AWED)
1250 24th St. NW, Room 120
Washington DC 20037
(202) 857-0091

CTA Management Group, Inc.
709 2nd St., Suite 1004
Washington DC 20002
(202) 543-1200

Wisconsin

Women's Business Initiative Corporation
3112 West Highland Blvd.
Milwaukee WI 53208
(414) 933-3231

Small Business Development Centers (SBDCs)

Call the office listed below for your state and a staff member will direct you to the SBDC closest to you. In Texas, call the regional office closest to you. For more information about training and counseling opportunities at SBDCs, see page 6.

Alabama

Alabama SBDC Consortium
University of Alabama at Birmingham
Medical Towers Bldg.
1717 11th Ave., Suite 419
Birmingham AL 35294
(205) 934-7260

Alaska

Alaska SBDC
University of Alaska at Anchorage
430 West Seventh Ave., Suite 110
Anchorage AK 99501
(907) 274-7232

Arizona

Arizona SBDC Network
2411 West 14th St., Suite 132
Tempe AZ 85251
(602) 731-8720

Arkansas

Arkansas SBDC
University of Arkansas at Little Rock
100 South Main, Suite 401
Little Rock AR 72201
(501) 324-9043

California

California SBDC Program
Department of Commerce
801 K St., Suite 1700
Sacramento CA 95814
(916) 324-5068

Colorado

Colorado SBDC
Colorado Office of Business Development
1625 Broadway, Suite 1710
Denver CO 80202
(303) 892-3809

Connecticut

Connecticut SBDC
University of Connecticut
368 Fairfield Road, U-41, Room 422
Storrs CT 06269-2041
(203) 486-4135

Delaware

Delaware SBDC
University of Delaware
Purnell Hall, Suite 005
Newark DE 19716-2711
(302) 831-2747

Florida

Florida SBDC Network
University of West Florida
11000 University Parkway
Pensacola FL 32514
(904) 444-2066

Georgia

Georgia SBDC
University of Georgia
Chicopee Complex, 1180 East Broad St.
Athens GA 30602-5412
(706) 542-5760

Hawaii

Hawaii SBDC Network
University of Hawaii at Hilo
523 West Lanikaula St.
Hilo HI 96720
(808) 933-3515

Idaho

Idaho SBDC
Boise State University
1910 University Drive
Boise ID 83725
(208) 385-1640

Illinois

Illinois SBDC
Dept. of Commerce and Community Affairs
620 East Adams St., 6th Floor
Springfield IL 62701
(217) 524-5856

Indiana

Indiana SBDC
Economic Development Council
One North Capitol, Suite 420
Indianapolis IN 46204
(317) 264-6871

Iowa

Iowa SBDC
Iowa State University
137 Lynn Ave.
Ames IA 50010
(515) 292-6351

Kansas

Kansas SBDC
Wichita State University
1845 Fairmount
Wichita KS 67260-0148
(316) 689-3193

Kentucky

Kentucky SBDC
University of Kentucky
Center for Business Development
225 Business & Economics Building
Lexington KY 40506-0034
(606) 257-7668

Louisiana

Louisiana SBDC
Northeast Louisiana University
College of Business Administration
700 University Ave.
Monroe LA 71209-6435
(318) 342-5506

Maine

Maine SBDC
University of Southern Maine
96 Falmouth St.
Portland ME 04103
(207) 780-4420

Maryland

Maryland SBDC
Dept. of Economic & Employment Development
217 East Redwood St., 10th Floor
Baltimore MD 21202
(410) 333-6995

Massachusetts

Massachusetts SBDC
Universit. of Massachusetts: Amherst
Room 205, School of Management
Amherst MA 01003
(413) 545-6301

Michigan

Michigan SBDC
2727 Second Ave.
Detroit MI 48201
(313) 577-4848

Minnesota

Minnesota SBDC
500 Metro Square, 121 7th Place East
St. Paul MN 55101-2146
(612) 297-5770

Mississippi

Mississippi SBDC
University of Mississippi
Old Chemistry Building, Suite 216
University MS 38677
(601) 232-5001

Missouri

Missouri SBDC
University of Missouri
300 University Place
Columbia MO 65211
(314) 882-0344

Montana

Montana SBDC
Montana Department of Commerce
1424 9th Ave.
Helena MT 59620
(406) 444-4780

Nebraska

Nebraska SBDC
University of Nebraska at Omaha
60th & Dodge Sts., CBA Room 407
Omaha NE 68182
(402) 554-2521

Nevada

Nevada SBDC
University of Nevada: Reno
College of Business Administration-032, Room 411
Reno NV 89557-0100
(702) 784-1717

New Hampshire

New Hampshire SBDC
University of New Hampshire
108 McConnell Hall
Durham NH 03824
(603) 862-2200

New Jersey

New Jersey SBDC
Rutgers University
Graduate School of Management
180 University Ave.
Newark NJ 07102
(201) 648-5950

New Mexico

New Mexico SBDC
Santa Fe Community College
P.O. Box 4187
Santa Fe NM 87502-4187
(505) 438-1362

New York

New York SBDC
State University of New York
SUNY Central Plaza, S-523
Albany NY 12246
(518) 443-5398

North Carolina

North Carolina SBDC
University of North Carolina
4509 Creedmoor Road, Suite 201
Raleigh NC 27612
(919) 571-4154

North Dakota

North Dakota SBDC
University of North Dakota
118 Gamble Hall, UND, Box 7308
Grand Fork ND 58202
(701) 777-3700

Ohio

Ohio SBDC
77 South High St., 28th Floor
P.O. Box 1001
Columbus OH 43226-0101
(614) 466-2711

Oklahoma

Oklahoma SBDC
Southeastern Oklahoma State University
P.O. Box 2584, Station A
Durant OK 74701
(405) 924-0277

Oregon

Oregon SBDC
Lane Community College
99 West 10th Ave., Suite 216
Eugene OR 97401
(503) 726-2250

Pennsylvania

Pennsylvania SBDC
The Wharton School
University of Pennsylvania
444 Vance Hall, 3733 Spruce St.
Philadelphia PA 19104-6374
(215) 898-1219

Puerto Rico

Puerto Rico SBDC
University of Puerto Rico
P.O. Box 5253 College Station
Mayaguez PR 00681
(809) 834-3590

Rhode Island

Rhode Island SBDC
Bryant College
1150 Douglas Pike
Smithfield RI 02917
(401) 232-6111

South Carolina

Small Business Development Center
University of South Carolina
College of Business Administration
Columbia SC 29201-9980
(803) 777-4907

South Dakota

South Dakota SBDC
University of South Dakota
414 East Clark
Vermillion SD 57069
(605) 677-5279

Tennessee

Tennessee SBDC
Memphis State University
Building 1, South Campus
Memphis TN 38152
(901) 678-2500

Texas

North Texas-Dallas SBDC
Bill J. Priest Institute for Economic Development
140 Corinth St.
Dallas TX 75215
(214) 565-5833

University of Houston SBDC
University of Houston
601 Jefferson, Suite 2330
Houston TX 77002
(713) 752-8444

NW Texas SBDC
Texas Tech University
2579 South Loop 289, Suite 114
Lubbock TX 79423
(806) 745-3973

UTSA South Texas Border SBDC
UTSA Downtown Center, 801 South Bowie St.
San Antonio TX 78205
(210) 558-2460

Utah

Utah Small Business Development Center
102 West 500 South, Suite 315
Salt Lake City UT 84101
(801) 581-7905

Vermont

Vermont SBDC
Vermont Technical College
P.O. Box 422
Randolph VT 05060
(802) 728-9101

Virgin Islands

UVI SBDC
University of the Virgin Islands
P.O. Box 1087
St. Thomas VI 00804
(809) 776-3206

Virginia

Virginia Small Business Development Center
1021 East Cary St., 11th Floor
Richmond VA 23219
(804) 371-8253

Washington DC

District of Columbia SBDC
Howard University
6th and Fairmont St. NW, Room 128
Washington DC 20059
(202) 806-1550

Washington

Washington SBDC
Washington State University
245 Todd Hall
Pullman WA 99164-4727
(509) 335-1576

Wisconsin

Wisconsin SBDC
University of Wisconsin
432 North Lake St., Room 423
Madison WI 53706
(608) 263-7794

Wyoming

WSBDC State Network Office
951 North Poplar
Casper WY 82601
(307) 235-4825

SCORE Women's Business Ownership Coordinators

To find a retired women executive who will provide free counseling on a range of business start-up and management issues, contact the coordinator that serves your state. For more information about SCORE, see pages 4-6.

These volunteer coordinators change frequently. If the coordinator on this list is no longer serving your area, contact the national liaison person listed below at the SBA Office of Women's Business Ownership for current information.

National Office, OWBO SCORE Liaison

Levora President
SBA Office of Women's Business Ownership
409 3rd St. SW, 6th Floor
Washington DC 20416
(202) 205-6673

Region 1

Maine, Vermont, Massachusetts, New Hampshire, Connecticut, Rhode Island

Aline Lotter
41 Brook St.
Manchester NH 03104
(603) 668-5166

Region 2

New York, New Jersey, Puerto Rico, Virgin Islands

This position was vacant at press time.

Region 3

Pennsylvania, Delaware, Maryland, Virginia West Virginia, Washington D.C.

Beatrice Checket
907 Sextant Way
Annapolis MD 21401
(4101) 266-8746

Region 4

North Carolina, South Carolina, Kentucky, Tennessee, Georgia, Alabama, Mississippi, Florida

Julie Mullane
141 Green Heron Court
Daytona Beach FL 32119
(904) 788-5350

Region 5
Minnesota, Wisconsin, Michigan, Ohio, Indiana, Illinois

Gwen Arnold
1923 Sheffield Drive
Ypsilanti MI 48198
(313) 483-1121

Region 6
New Mexico, Texas, Oklahoma, Arkansas, Louisiana

Doris Bentley
222 Amelia St.
Lafayette LA 70506
(318) 232-2970

Region 7
Kansas, Missouri, Iowa, Nebraska

Rose Krisinger
11145 Mill Valley Road
Omaha NE 68154
(402) 221-3604

Region 8
Montana, N. Dakota, S. Dakota, Wyoming, Utah, Colorado

Jo Steele
7630 Pine Oak Lane
Colorado Springs CO 80926
(719) 576-0732

Region 9
California, Nevada, Arizona, Hawaii

Betty Williamson
525 East St. Louis, #406
Las Vegas NV 89104
(702) 734-6211

Region 10
Washington, Oregon, Idaho, Alaska

Diana Wilhite
617 N. Helena
Spokane WA 99202
(509) 534-9001

Minority Business Development Agency (MBDA) Regional Offices

To find out about minority business assistance in your area, contact the office that serves your state or area. For general information about MBDA programs, contact the Washington D.C. office and review the information on MBDAs on page 8.

For General Information

U.S. Department of Commerce
Minority Business Development Agency
Communications Division
Room 5073
Washington DC 20230
(202) 482-1936

Atlanta Region

Alabama, Florida, Georgia, Kentucky, Mississippi, North Carolina, South Carolina, Tennessee

MBDA Regional Office
401 West Peachtree St. NW, Suite 1715
Atlanta GA 30308-3516
(404) 730-3300

MBDA Miami District Officer
51 Southwest 1st Ave.
Room 1314, Box 25
Miami FL 33130
(305) 536-5054

Chicago Region

Illinois, Indiana, Iowa, Kansas, Michigan, Minnesota, Missouri, Nebraska, Ohio, Wisconsin

MBDA Regional Office
55 East Monroe St., Suite 1440
Chicago IL 60603
(312) 353-0182

Chicago Mega Center
105 West Adams St., 7th Floor
Chicago IL 60603
(312) 977-9190

Dallas Region

Arkansas, Colorado, Louisiana, Montana, New Mexico, North Dakota, Oklahoma, South Dakota, Texas, Utah, Wyoming

MBDA Regional Office
1100 Commerce St., Room 7B23
Dallas TX 75242
(214) 767-8001

San Francisco Region

Alaska, American Samoa, Arizona, California, Hawaii, Idaho, Nevada, Oregon, Washington

MBDA Regional Office
221 Main St., Room 1280
San Francisco CA 94105
(415) 744-3001

MBDA Los Angeles District Office
9660 Flair Drive, Suite 455
El Monte CA 91731
(818) 453-8636

Washington Region

Delaware, Maryland, Pennsylvania, Virginia, Washington DC, West Virginia

MBDA Regional Office
1255 22nd St. NW, Suite 701
Washington DC 20036
(202) 377-1356

MBDA Philadelphia District
600 Arch St., Room 10128
Philadelphia PA 19106
(215) 597-9236

New York Region

Connecticut, Maine, Massachusetts, New Hampshire, New Jersey, New York, Puerto Rico, Rhode Island, Vermont, Virgin Islands

MBDA Regional Office
26 Federal Plaza, Room 3720
New York NY 10278
(212) 264-3262

MBDA Boston District Office
10 Causeway St., Room 418
Boston MA 02222-1041
(617) 565-6850

Women's Bureau: U.S. Department of Labor Regional Offices

For information about bureau programs in your area, contact the regional office that serves your state. For general information about the bureau, contact the Washington D.C. office at the address below. For more information about the bureau, see page 10.

Federal Office

Women's Bureau, Office of the Secretary
U.S. Department of Labor
200 Constitution Ave., NW
Washington DC 20210
(202) 219-8913

Region 1

Connecticut, Maine, Massachusetts, New Hampshire, Rhode Island, Vermont

Women's Bureau
One Congress St.
Boston MA 02114
(617) 565-1988

Region 2

New York, New Jersey, Puerto Rico, Virgin Islands

Women's Bureau
201 Varick St., Room 601
New York NY 10014
(212) 337-2389

Region 3

Delaware, Washington D.C., Maryland, Pennsylvania, Virginia, West Virginia

Women's Bureau
3535 Market St.,
Gateway Building, Room 2450
Philadelphia PA 19104
(215) 596-1183

Region 4

Alabama, Florida, Georgia, Kentucky, Mississippi, North Carolina, South Carolina, Tennessee

Women's Bureau
1371 Peachtree St. NE, Room 323
Atlanta GA 30367
(404) 347-4461

Region 5

Illinois, Indiana, Michigan, Minnesota, Ohio, Wisconsin

Women's Bureau
230 S. Dearborn St., Room 1022
Chicago IL 60604
(312) 353-6985

Region 6

Arkansas, Louisiana, New Mexico, Oklahoma, Texas

Women's Bureau
Federal Building
525 Griffin St., Suite 731
Dallas TX 75202
(214) 767-6985

Region 7

Iowa, Kansas, Missouri, Nebraska

Women's Bureau
911 Walnut St., Room 2511
Kansas City MO 64106
(816) 426-6108

Region 8

Colorado, Montana, North Dakota, South Dakota, Utah, Wyoming

Women's Bureau
1801 California St., Suite 905
Denver CO 80202-2614
(303) 391-6755

Region 9

Arizona, California, Hawaii, Nevada

Women's Bureau
71 Stevenson St., Suite 927
San Francisco CA 94105
(415) 744-6679

Region 10

Alaska, Idaho, Oregon, Washington

Women's Bureau
1111 Third Ave., Room 885
Seattle WA 98101-3211
(206) 553-1534

First-Stop State Offices

Contact the office in your state for information about local and state business development opportunities. For more information about what first-stop offices do, see page 31.

Alabama

The State of Alabama offers no specific programs for women-owned business enterprises. The State does assist WBEs as part of its minority business assistance program.

Alabama Development Office
Office of Minority Business Enterprise
State of Alabama
Alabama Development Office
Alabama Center for Commerce
401 Adams Ave.
Montgomery AL 36130
(205) 242-0400 or (800) 248-0033

Alaska

The State of Alaska has no specific office of women's business ownership assistance. The University of Alaska Small Business Development Center does offer several programs for women business owners.

University of Alaska Small Business Development Center
430 West Seventh Ave., Suite 110
Anchorage AK 99501
(907) 274-7232

Arizona

State of Arizona Governor's Office for Women
Governor's Office for Women
1700 West Washington #240
Phoenix AZ 85007
(602) 542-1755

California

Office of Small and Minority Business
1531 I St., Second Floor
Sacramento CA 95814-2016
(916) 322-1847

Colorado

Colorado Office of Business Development
Small Business Office
Colorado Women's Business Program
1625 Broadway Suite 1710
Denver CO 80282
(303) 892-3840

Connecticut

The Connecticut Department of Economic Development provides assistance to WBEs and administers a program to encourage the participation of WBEs in state procurement.

Small Business Services
Connecticut Department of Economic Development
865 Brook St.
Rocky Hill CT 06067-3405
(203) 258-4275

Delaware

Delaware has no specific programs designed to assist women business owners.

Florida

Florida Department of Commerce
Small and Minority Business Advocacy Office
107 West Gaines St.
516 Collins Building
Tallahassee FL 32399-2000
(904) 487-4698

Georgia

The State of Georgia has no specific programs for women business owners. However, the Georgia Department of Administrative Services sponsors a program to encourage the participation of women and minority businesses in state procurement.

Small and Minority Business Program
Georgia Department of Administrative Services
200 Piedmont Ave., Suite 1302
Atlanta GA 30334
(404) 656-6315

Hawaii

The State of Hawaii has no specific programs for women business owners. However, the Office of Small Business Information Services can provide women with general information on state resources for business start-up and expansion.

Department of Business and Economic Development
Small Business Information Services
220 S. King St.
Honolulu HI 96804
(808) 587-2600

Illinois

The State of Illinois has a full-time women's business advocacy program in its office of Small and Minority Business Advocacy.

Illinois Department of Commerce and Community Affairs
Small and Minority Business Advocacy
State of Illinois Center
100 West Randolph St., Suite 3-400
Chicago IL 60601
(312) 814-7176 or (800) 252-2923

Indiana

Indiana assists women business owners through the Office of Women and Minorities in Business.

Indiana Small Business Development Corporation
Office of Women and Minorities in Business
One North Capitol Ave., Suite 1275
Indianapolis IN 46204-2026
(317) 264-2820

Iowa

Iowa assists WBEs through the State Department of Economic Development.

Iowa Department of Economic Development
Small Business Bureau Development
200 East Grand Ave.
Des Moines IA 50309
(515) 242-4813

Kansas

Kansas assists WBEs as part of its minority business development program.

Office of Minority Business
Kansas Department of Commerce
700 SW Harrison, Suite 1300
Topeka KS 66603-3712
(913) 296-3805

Kentucky

Kentucky Small Business Office assists women business owners as part of its overall small business advocacy program.

Kentucky Cabinet for Economic Development
Small Business Assistance Division
Capitol Plaza Tower, 23rd Floor
Frankfort KY 40601
(502) 564-2064 or (800) 626-2930

Maine

The state of Maine does not have a state-sponsored agency or program to assist women business owners. The Women's Business Development Corporation, a private non-profit organization serves as an information resource to women business owners in the state.

The Women's Business Development Corp.
P.O. Box 658
Bangot ME 04402
(207) 234-2019

Maryland

The state of Maryland offers no programs specifically to assist women business owners. However, the Maryland Department of Transportation provides some assistance to women business owners through its Minority Business Enterprise Program.

Maryland Department of Transportation
Minority Business Development Program
P.O. Box 8755
Elm Road, BWI Airport
Baltimore MD 21240
(410) 859-7327

Massachusetts

The Massachusetts State Office of Minority and Women's Business Assistance offers several programs to assist women business owners.

**Office of Minority and Women
Business Assistance**
100 Cambridge St., Room 1305
Boston MA 02202
(617) 727-8692

Michigan

Massachusetts has no specific programs for women business owners. However the transportation department offers procurement assistance to women business owners through its Office of Small Business Liaison.

Michigan Department of Transportation
Office of Small Business Liaison
Transportation Building
425 West Ottawa
Lansing MI 48909
(517) 373-2090

Minnesota

Minnesota sponsors an office of women's business advocacy in partnership with the U.S. Small Business Administration and Winona State University.

Winona State University
Minnesota Small Business Development Center
Women in Business Advocate Division
P. O. Box 5838
Winona MN 55987-5838
(507) 457-5088

Mississippi

Mississippi assists women business owners as part of its entrepreneurial development program.

**Mississippi Department of Economic and
Community Development**
Office of Minority Business Enterprise
Minority and Women's Advocacy Program
Box 849
Jackson MS 39205
(601) 359-3448

Missouri

The Missouri Council on Women's Economic Development and Training serves as the state's women's business advocate.

Missouri Department of Economic Development
Council on Women's Economic Development
P.O. Box 1684
Jefferson City MO 65102-1684
(314) 751-3237

Nebraska

Nebraska has no specific programs for women business owners. The Department of Economic Development does maintain a directory of women-owned businesses.

Nebraska Department of Economic Development
Existing Business Assistance Division
P.O. Box 94666
Lincoln NE 68509
(402) 471-3782 or(800) 426-6505

Nevada

The Nevada Office of Small Business Women's Business Advocacy program assists women business owners and monitors the State's efforts to assist WBEs.

Commission on Economic Development
Women's Business Advocacy Program
Office of Small Business
3770 Howard Hughes Parkway, Suite 295
Las Vegas NV 89158
(702) 486-7282

New Jersey

The New Jersey Division of Women and Minority Businesses offers a comprehensive program of assistance for women business owners.

**New Jersey Department of Commerce
and Economic Development**
Division of Development for Small, Women
and Minority Businesses
20 West State St., CN 835
Trenton NJ 08625-0835
(609) 292-3862

New Mexico

The State of New Mexico sponsors a program to encourage women business owners to participate in state procurement.

State of New Mexico
General Services Department
State Purchasing Division
Procurement Assistance Program
1100 St. Francis Drive
Santa Fe NM 87503
(505) 827-0425

New York

The New York Office of Women's Business Development assists women business owners and administers a state-wide unified women's business certification program.

New York State Office of Minority and Women's Business Development
1 Commerce Plaza
Albany NY 12245
(518) 474-6346

North Carolina

The North Carolina Department of Administration sponsors a program to encourage women business owners to participate in State procurement.

Department of Administration
Division of Purchase and Contract
Administration Building
116 West Jones St.
Raleigh NC 27603-8002
(919) 733-8965

North Dakota

The North Dakota Department of Development and Finance has specialized programs to help women business owners.

Department of Economic Development and Finance
1833 E. Bismarck Expressway
Bismarck ND 58504
(701) 221-5300 Ext. 5342

Ohio

The State of Ohio offers comprehensive assistance to women business owners through its Women's Business Resource Program.

Economic Development Division Office
Office of Small and Minority Business
Ohio Small Business Development Center
Women's Business Resource Program, SBDC
P.O. Box 1001 or
28th Floor Vern Riffe Center
77 South High St.
Columbus OH 43215
(614) 466-4945 or (800) 848-1300

Oklahoma

In Oklahoma, the Office of Women-Owned Businesses sponsors a number of programs to assist women with business development.

Oklahoma Department of Commerce
Business Development Division
Office of Women-Owned Business Assistance
P. O. Box 26980
Oklahoma City OK 73126-0980
(405) 841-5242

Oregon

The State of Oregon has no specific office of women's business advocacy. It does assist women business owners as part of its minority business assistance program.

Oregon Executive Department
Office of Minority, Women and Emerging Small Business
155 Cottage St. NE, Third Floor
Salem OR 97310
(503) 373-1241

Pennsylvania

The Pennsylvania Department of Commerce Women's Business Development Program serves as the women's business advocate for the State. This office maintains statistics, certifies WBEs and assists WBEs in locating resources.

Pennsylvania Department of Commerce
Bureau of Women's Business Development Program
400 Forum Building
Harrisburg PA 17120
(717) 787-3339

Pennsylvania Office of Minority and Women Business Enterprise
Room 502 North Office Building
Harrisburg PA 17125
(717) 787-7380

Rhode Island

The Office of Minority Business Assistance assists WBEs as part of its minority business development program.

**Rhode Island Department
of Economic Development**
Office of Minority Business Assistance
7 Jackson Walkway
Providence RI 02903
(401) 277-2601

South Carolina

The State of South Carolina has no specific programs. The Office of Small and Minority Business assistance does provide resources to women business owners.

Office of the Governor
Office of Small and Minority Business Assistance
1205 Pendleton St.
Columbia SC 29201
(803) 734-0657

Tennessee

The State of Tennessee offers no specific programs. The Office of Minority Business Enterprise does assist women as part of its disadvantaged business program.

**Department of Economic and
Community Development**
Office of Minority Business Enterprise
Small Business Office
Rachel Jackson Building, 7th Floor
320 Sixth Ave. North
Nashville TN 37243-0405
(615) 741-2545

Texas

The State of Texas has no specific office of women's business ownership. Several state offices do sponsor programs to assist women business owners in competing for procurement contracts.

State of Texas Department of Commerce
State Purchasing and General Services Commission
P. O. Box 13047
Austin TX 78711-3047
(512) 463-3416

Utah

The Utah Women's Business Development Council and the Utah Small Business Development Center offer special assistance to encourage the development of women-owned businesses.

Utah Small Business Development Center
Women's Business Development Council
102 W. 500th St. South, Suite 315
Salt Lake City UT 84104
(801) 295-3668

Vermont

There are no specific state-wide programs in Vermont designed to assist women business owners. However, the State and the City of Burlington in partnership with Trinity College jointly fund the Women's Small Business Project.

The Women's Small Business Project
Trinity College
208 Colchester Ave.
Burlington VT 05401
(802) 658-0337

Washington

The State of Washington assists women business entrepreneurs as part of its program to encourage the development of minority businesses.

**State of Washington Office of Minority and
Women's Business Enterprises**
406 South Water
P.O. Box 41160
Olympia WA 98504-1160
(206) 753-9693

West Virginia

Women business owners should contact the rural business development specialist for assistance.

Rural Business Development Specialist
West Virginia Business Development Center
1115 Virginia St. East
Charleston WV 25301
(304) 558-2960

Wisconsin

The State of Wisconsin assists women business owners through its Department of Development. Within the Department, the Office of Women's Business Services serves as an advocate for women's business issues and offers resources and financial programs designed to assist WBEs.

Wisconsin Department of Development
Bureau of Business Development
Women's Business Services
123 West Washington Ave.
P. O. Box 7970
Madison WI 53707
(608) 266-0593

Wyoming

The State of Wyoming has no specific programs for women but does offer general small business development assistance through the Department of Commerce.

Department of Commerce
Division of Economic and Community Development
The Barrett Building, Fourth Floor
Cheyenne WY 82002
(307) 777-7284

Resources, Programs and Agencies

Office of Small and Disadvantaged Business Utilization (OSDBU)

Contact the women's business representative or small business specialist in each of the federal departments below for information about selling your goods or services to federal agencies. For more information about OSDBU programs, see page 47.

Major Government Departments

Agriculture Department
14th and Independence Ave. SW
1323 South Bldg.
Washington DC 20250-9400
(202) 720-7117

Air Force Department
The Pentagon, Room 5E271
Washington DC 20330-1000
(703) 697-1950

Army Department
The Pentagon, Room 2A712
Washington DC 20301-0106
(703) 695-9800

Commerce Department
14th and Constitution Ave. NW, H6411
Washington DC 20230
(202) 482-1472

Defense Department
The Pentagon, Room 2A340
Washington DC 20301-3061
(703) 697-4912

Defense Logistics Agency
Cameron Station
5010 Duke St, Room 4B130
Alexandria VA 22304-6100
(703) 274-6471

Education Department
400 Maryland Ave.
Room 3120 (ROB #3)
Washington DC 20202-0521
(202) 708-9820

Energy Department
1707 H. St. NW, Room 904
Washington DC 20585
(202) 254-5583

Environmental Protection Agency
401 M St. SW, A-149-C
Washington DC 20460
(703) 305-7305

General Services Administration
18th and F Sts. NW, Room 6029
Washington DC 20405
(202) 501-1021

Health and Human Services Department
200 Independence Ave. SW, Room 517D
Washington DC 20201
(202) 690-7300

Housing and Urban Development Department
451 7th St. SW, Room 10232
Washington DC 20410
(202) 708-1428

Interior Department
1849 C St. NW, Room 2747
Washington DC 20240
(202) 208-3493

Justice Department
Room 3225 Ariel Rios Bldg
12th and Pennsylvania Ave. NW
Washington DC 20530
(202) 616-0521

Labor Department
200 Constitution Ave. NW, Room C-2318
Washington DC 20210
(202) 219-9148

National Aeronautics and Space Administration (NASA)
300 E. St. SW
Room 1T70, FB-10B-Code K
Washington DC 20546
(202) 358-2088

Navy Department
2211 Jefferson Davis Highway
Crystal Plaza, Building 5, Room 120

Arlington VA 20360-5000
(703) 602-2695

State Department
1701 Fort Meyer Dr., Room 633 (SA-6)
Rossyln VA 22209
(703) 875-6824

Transportation Department
400 7th St. SW, Room 9414
Washington DC 20590
(202) 366-1930

Treasury Department
15th and Pennsylvania Ave. NW
Room 6100, The Annex
Washington DC 20220
(202) 622-0530

Veteran Affairs Department
810 Vermont Ave. NW
OSDBU 005SB
Washington DC 20420
(202) 376-6996

Other Government Agencies

Action
1100 Vermont Ave NW, Room 2101
Washington DC 20525
(202) 606-6150

Administrative Office of U.S. Courts
1120 Vermont Ave. NW, Room 907
Washington DC 20544
(202) 633-6299

Agency For International Development
1100 Wilson Blvd.
(SA-14) Room 1200A
Arlington VA 20523-1414
(703) 875-1551

Commodity Futures Trading Commission
2033 K St. NW, Room 205
Washington DC 20581
(202) 254-9735

Consumer Product Safety Commission
5401 Westbard Ave., Room 240
Bethesda MD 20816
(301) 492-6621

Corps of Engineers
Pulaski Bldg., Room 4117
20 Massachusetts Ave. NW
Washington DC 20314
(202) 272-0725

Defense Nuclear Agency
6801 Telegraph Rd.
Alexandria VA 22310-3398
(703) 325-5021

Executive Office Of The President
Office Of Administration
New Executive Office Bldg., Room 5001
725 17th St. NW
Washington DC 20503
(202) 395-3314

Export-Import Bank Of The U.S.
811 Vermont Ave. NW, Room 1107
Washington DC 20571
(202) 566-7548

Farm Credit Administration
1501 Farm Credit Drive, Room 1215
McLean VA 22102-5090
(703) 883-4147

Federal Communications Commission
1919 M St. NW, Room 408
Washington DC 20554
(202) 634-1530

Federal Emergency Management Agency
Office of Acquisitions
Federal Center Plaza
500 C St. SW, Room 726
Washington DC 20472
(202) 646-3744

Federal Maritime Commission
1100 L St. NW, Room 10409
Washington DC 20573
(202) 523-5900

Federal Mediation And Conciliation Service
2100 K St. NW, Room 100
Washington DC 20427
(202) 653-5310

Federal Trade Commission
6th and Pennsylvania Ave. NW, Room 702
Washington DC 20580
(202) 326-2260 or 2258

Federal Transit Administration
400 7th St. SW, Room 7412
Washington DC 20590
(202) 366-2285

General Accounting Office
441 S. St. NW, Room 2001
Washington DC 20001
(202) 275-3550

Government Printing Office
North Capitol and H Sts. NW
Room C-897
Washington DC 20401
(202) 512-1365

International Trade Commission
500 E St. SW, 214A
Washington DC 20436
(202) 205-2730

Interstate Commerce Commission
12th and Constitution Ave. NW, Room 1319
Washington DC 20423
(202) 927-5370 or 5975

Library of Congress
1701 Brightseat Rd.
Landover MD 20785
(202) 707-8616

Marine Corps
3033 Wilson Blvd.
Clarendon Square Bldg.
Arlington VA 22202
(703) 696-1022

National Academy of Science
Office of Contracts and Grants
2001 Wisconsin Ave. NW, Room 406
Washington DC 20007
(202) 344-2254

National Archives And Records Administration
8th St. and Pennsylvania Ave. NW, Room 406
Washington DC 20408
(202) 501-5110

National Endowments For The Humanities
1100 Pennsylvania Ave. NW, Room 202
Washington DC 20506
(202) 786-0233

National Labor Relations Board
1099 14th St. NW, Suite 6100
Washington DC 20570
(202) 273-4210

National Science Foundation
1800 G St. NW, Room 1250-J
Washington DC 20550
(202) 653-5202 or 5335

Nuclear Regulatory Commission
Maryland National Bank Bldg., R7217
7735 Old Georgetown Rd.
Bethesda MD 20555
(301) 492-4665

Office Of Personnel Management
1900 E St. NW, Room 1452
Washington DC 20415
(202) 606-2180

Overseas Private Investment Corp.
Sumner Square
1615 M St. NW
Washington DC 20527
(202) 457-7080

Peace Corps
1990 K. St. NW, Room 6368
Washington DC 20526
(202) 606-3513

Pennsylvania Ave. Development Corporation
1331 Pennsylvania Ave. NW, Suite 1220 North
Washington DC 20004-1703
(202) 724-9091

U.S. Postal Service
475 L'Enfant Plaza West SW
Room 3641
Washington DC 20260-5616
(202) 268-6578

Railroad Retirement Board
1310 G. St. NW, Suite 800
Washington DC 20005
(202) 272-7742

Resolution Trust Corporation
801 17th St. NW
Washington DC 20434-0001
(202) 272-7742

Securities And Exchange Commission
450 8th St. NW, Room 9138
Washington DC 20549
(202) 272-2644

Small Business Administration
Small Purchase and Contracts
409 3rd St. SW, 5th Floor
Washington DC 20416
(202) 205-6622

Smithsonian Institution
995 L'Enfant Plaza SW, Room 3120
Washington DC 20560
(202) 287-3508

Tennessee Valley Authority
Chestnut St., Tower 2
P.O. Box 11127
Chattanooga TN 37401-2127
(615) 751-6267

U. S. Information Agency
330 C St. SW, Room 1617
HHS, South Bldg.
Washington DC 20547
(202) 205-5404

Washington Metropolitan Area
Transit Authority Metro
600 5th St. NW
Washington DC 20001
(202) 962-1082

Office of Procurement
Procurement and Operations
14th and Constitution Ave NW, H6516
Washington DC 20230
(202) 482-555 or 1472

Patent & Trademark Office
Office of Procurement
2011 Crystal Drive
Crystal Park #1, Suite 810
Arlington VA 22202
(703) 305-8152

National Oceanic and Atmospheric Administration
Systems Program Office
Procurement Staff
Room 9626, Code SPD-X2
Silver Spring MD 20910
(301) 713-3478

National Oceanic and Atmospheric Administration
Fleet Replacement and Modernization
Contracts Office, Suite 2010
2611 Jefferson Davis Hwy.
Arlington VA 22202
(703) 602-9049

National Oceanic and Atmospheric Administration
Procurement Operations Division
1325 East West Hwy.
Room 4301, Code 0A31
Silver Spring MD 20910
(301) 731-0847

Census Bureau
Procurement Office
Federal Office Bldg. #3, Room 1551
Suitland MD 20233
(301) 763-1954

National Institute of Standards and Technology (NIST)
Systems Program Office
Acquisition and Assistance Division
Quince Orchard and Hwy. 270
Bldg. 301, Room B-132
Gaithersburg MD 20899
(301) 975-6343

Advanced Technology Program (ATP)
AA S. Admin. Bldg. - NIST
Gaithersburg MD 20899-0001
(301) 975-5187

National Technical Information Service (NTIS)
Contracting Service Division
Forbes Bldg., Room 209
5285 Port Royal Rd.
Springfield VA 22161
(202) 482-1472

Small Business Innovation Research
1315 East-West Highway
SSMC3 Station 15342, Code CS/RT
Silver Spring MD 20910
(301) 713-3565

State Departments of Transportation

For information about certification as a women's business enterprise (WBE) contact your state department of transportation. See pages 47 and 52 for more information about the role of transportation departments in helping you sell goods and services to federal, state and local governments.

Alabama

State Transportation Department
Equipment and Procurement Office
Bureau of Human Resources
1409 Coliseum Blvd.
Montgomery AL 36130-3050
(800) 247-3618

Alaska

Department of Transportation
Public Facilities
Statewide DBE/EXEEO Office
P.O. Box 196900
Anchorage AK 99519-6900
(907) 266-1488

Arizona

Department of Transportation
Highway Division
1739 West Jackson St.
Mail Drop 100P
Phoenix AZ 85007
(602) 255-7211

Arkansas

Arkansas State Highway and Transportation Department
Programs and Contracts Division
P. O. Box 2261
Little Rock, AR 72203
(501) 569-2261

California

California Department of Transportation
Disadvantaged Business Enterprise Program
1120 North St.
P. O. Box 942873
Sacramento CA 94273-0001
(916) 654-4576

Colorado

Colorado Department of Transportation
Disadvantaged Business Certification Program
1560 Broadway, Suite 1530
Denver CO 80202
(303) 894-2355

Connecticut

Department of Transportation
2800 Berlin Turnpike
Newington CT 06111
(203) 594-2000

Delaware

Delaware Department of Transportation
Disadvantaged Business Enterprise Program
Contracts Administration Bldg.
P. O. Box 778
Dover DE 19903
(302) 739-4359

Florida

Florida Department of Transportation
Minority Programs Office
605 Suwannee St., M.S. 65
Room 260
Tallahassee FL 32399-0450
(904) 488-3145

Georgia

Transportation Department
Contracts Administration Office
2 Capitol Square
Atlanta GA 30334
(404) 656-5325

Hawaii

Department of Transportation
869 Punchbowl St.
Honolulu HI 96813
(808) 587-2150

Idaho

Idaho Transportation Department
P. O. Box 7129
Boise ID 83707-1129
(208) 334-8000

Illinois

Illinois Department of Transportation
Small Business Enterprises
2300 S. Dirksen Parkway, Room 319
DOT Administration Building
Springfield IL 62764
217-785-5947

Indiana

Indiana Department of Highways
Supportive Services
100 North Senate Ave., Room N8155
Indianapolis IN 46204
(317) 232-5093

Iowa

Department of Transportation
Contracts Office
800 Lincoln Way
Ames IA 50010
(515) 239-1414

Kansas

Kansas Department of Transportation
Office of Engineering Support
Docking State Office Building
7th Floor
Topeka KS 66612
(913) 296-7940

Kentucky

Highway Department
Contracts Procurement Division
501 High St.
Frankfort KY 40622
(502) 564-3500

Louisiana

Department of Transportation and Development
Post Office Box 94245
Baton Rouge LA 70804-9245
Attn: Compliance Programs Section
(504) 379-1382

Maine

Department of Transportation
Division of Equal Opportunity
and Employee Relations
Transportation Building
State House Station 16
Augusta ME 04333-0016
(207) 287-3576

Maryland

Department of Transportation
MBE-EOO
P.O. Box 8755
BWI Airport
Baltimore MD 21240
(410) 859-7327

Michigan

Michigan Department of Transportation
Disadvantaged Business Enterprise Program
Bureau of Administration
Office of Small Business Liaison
Transportation Building
425 West Ottawa
Lansing MI 48913
(517) 373-2090

Minnesota

Minnesota Department of Transportation
Disadvantaged Business Program
EEO Contract Management Office
395 John Ireland Blvd.
123 Transportation Building
St. Paul MN 55155
(612) 297-1376

Mississippi

Mississippi State Highway Department
Procurement Division
P. O. Box 1850
Jackson MS 39215-1850
(601) 359-1165

Missouri

Highway and Transportation Department
Equipment and Procurement Division
P.O. Box 270
Jefferson City MO 65102
(314) 751-3720

Montana

Montana Department of Highways
Civil Rights Bureau
2701 Prospect Ave.
P.O. Box 201001
Helena MT 59620-1001
(406) 444-6337

Nebraska

Nebraska Department of Roads
Procurement
Central Complex Headquarters
1500 Highway 2, Room 105
Lincoln NE 68509
(402) 479-4528

Nevada

Nevada Department of Transportation
Contracts Compliance
1263 South Stewart St.
Carson City NV 89712
(702) 687-5497

New Hampshire

New Hampshire Department of Transportation
John O. Morton Building
Compliance
Hazen Drive
P.O. Box 483
Concord NH 03302-0483
(603) 271-6611

New Jersey

Transportation Department
Procurement Division
CN 600, 1035 Pkwy. Ave., CN 605
Trenton NJ 08625
(609) 530-6355

New Mexico

Highway and Transportation Department
Procurement Bureau
P.O. Box 1149
Santa Fe NM 87504
(505) 827-5602

New York

Transportation Department
Contracts Management Bureau
Bldg. 5, Room 108
1220 Washington Ave.
Albany NY 12232
(518) 457-2600

North Carolina

Transportation Department
Purchasing
P.O. Box 25201
Raleigh NC 27611
(919) 733-7101

North Dakota

Department of Transportation
Civil Rights Office
608 East Boulevard Ave.
Bismarck ND 58505-0700
(701) 224-2576

Ohio

Ohio Department of Transportation
Office of Equal Opportunity
25 South Front St., Room 708
Columbus OH 43216
(614) 466-1163

Oklahoma

Oklahoma Department of Transportation
DBE Supportive Services
200 NE 21st St.
Oklahoma City OK 73105
(405) 521-3379

Oregon

Transportation Department
Program Section
307 Transportation Bldg
355 Capitol St. NE
Salem OR 97310
(503) 378-6546

Pennsylvania

Pennsylvania Department of Transportation
Bureau of Equal Opportunity
Room 109
Transportation Building
Harrisburg PA 17120
(717) 787-5891

Rhode Island

Transportation Department
Director's Office
210 State Office Bldg.
Providence RI 02903
(401) 277-2481

South Carolina

South Carolina Department of Highways and Public Transportation
Disadvantaged Business Enterprise Program
P. O. Box 191
Columbia SC 29202
(803) 737-1372

South Dakota

Department of Transportation
Civil Rights Program
700 Broadway Ave. East
Pierre SD 57501-2586
(605) 773-4906 or (605) 773-3284

Tennessee

Transportation Department
Contracts Certification Office
505 Deaderick St., Suite 700
Nashville TN 37243
(615) 741- 7929

Texas

State Department of Highways and Public Transportation
125 East 11th
Austin TX 78701-2483
(512) 463-8585

Utah

Transportation Department
4501 S. 2700 West
Salt Lake City UT 84119
(801) 965-4113

Vermont

Transportation Agency
133 State St.
Montpellier VT 05633
(802) 828-2661

Virginia

Commonwealth of Virginia
Department of Transportation
Office of Equal Opportunity
1401 East Broad St.
Richmond VA 23219
(804) 786-2935

Washington

Transportation Department
Office of Equal Opportunity
Transportation Bldg.
P.O. Box 47314
Olympia WA 98504-7314
(206) 705-7090

West Virginia

Transportation Department
Highway Division/Procurement Division
1900 Kanawha Blvd.
Charleston WV 25305
(304) 558-2908

Wisconsin

Wisconsin Department of Transportation
DBM/BMS
4802 Sheboygan Ave.
P.O. Box 7915
Madison WI 52707-7915
(608) 267-7721

Wyoming

Transportation Department
Purchasing Office
P.O. Box 1708
Cheyenne WY 82003
(307) 777-4487

Procurement Technical Assistance Centers

Most states have at least one procurement assistance center to help businesses sell to federal, state and local agencies. Check the state-by-state listing below to see if there is an office in your state. Only lead offices are listed here. In states where there are also satellite offices, the lead office will direct you to the center closest to you. For more information about these centers, see page 52.

Alabama

University of Alabama at Birmingham
V.P. Research & University Affairs
1717 11th Ave. S, Suite 419
Birmingham AL 35294-4410
(205) 934-7260

Alaska

University of Alaska Anchorage
Small Business Development Center
430 West 17th Ave., Suite 110
Anchorage AK 99501
(907) 274-7232

Arizona

APTAN, Inc.
360 North Hayden Road
Scottsdale AZ 85257
(602) 945-5452

National Center for American Indian Enterprise Development
National Center Headquarters
953 East Juanita Ave.
Mesa AZ 85204
(602) 831-7524

Arkansas

University of Arkansas
College of Business/ESC
120 Ozark Hall
Fayetteville AR 72701
(501) 686-2509

California

De Anza College/Business Division
c/o AMD, Procurement Assistance Center
Mail Stop 31
Sunnyvale CA 94088-3453
(408) 739-6283

Merced County Dept. of Economic & Strategic Development
Calif. Central Valley Contract Procurement Center
1632 N St.
Merced CA 95340
(209) 385-7657

Private Industry Council of Imperial County
1411 State St.
El Centro CA 92243
(619) 353-5050

Colorado

Colorado Office of Business Development
Governor's Office
1625 Broadway, Suite 1710
Denver CO 80202
(303) 892-3809

Connecticut

Southeast Area Technical Development Center
1084 Shennecossett Road
Groton CT 06340
(203) 449-8777

Delaware

Delaware State College
School of Business & Economics
1200 North Dupont Way
Dover DE 19901
(302) 739-3521

Florida

University of West Florida
11000 University Parkway
Procurement Technical Assistance
Pensacola FL 32514
(904) 474-2919

Georgia

Columbus College
Division of Continuing Education
Procurement Technical Assistance
Columbus GA 31993-2399
(706) 649-1092

**Center for Procurement
Technical Assistance**
One Arsenal Place
901 Front Ave., Suite 106
Columbus GA 31901-2727
(404) 649-1092

Georgia Tech Research Corporation
GA Institute of Technology
Procurement Assistance Center
Centennial Research Bldg., Room 246
Atlanta GA 30332-0420
(404) 894-6121

Hawaii

State of Hawaii
Dept. of Business, Economic Development & Tourism
Procurement Technical Assistance
P.O. Box 2359
Honolulu HI 96804
(808) 586-2598

Idaho

Idaho Dept. of Commerce
State of Idaho
Procurement Technical Assistance
700 West State St.
Boise ID 83720
(208) 334-2470

Illinois

Black Hawk College District
Black Hawk College Outreach
6600 34th Ave.
Moline IL 61265
(309) 752-0262

Latin American Chamber of Commerce
The Chicago PTA
2539 North Kedzie Ave., Suite 11
Chicago IL 60647
(312) 252-5211

State of Illinois
Dept. of Commerce & Community Affairs
Procurement Technical Assistance
620 East Adams St., 3rd Floor
Springfield IL 62701
(217) 524-0158

Indiana

Indiana Small Business Development Corp.
Government Marketing Assistance
One North Capital, Suite 1240
Indianapolis IN 46204-2026
(317) 264-5600

Partners in Contracting Corp.
8149 Kennedy Ave.
Highland IN 46322
(219) 923-8181

Iowa

State of Iowa
Dept. of Economic Development
Procurement Technical Assistance
200 East Grand Ave.
Des Moines IA 50309
(319) 398-5665

Kentucky

Cabinet for Economic Development
Dept. of Community Development
500 Mero St.
22nd Floor, Capital Plaza
Frankfort KY 40601
(800) 626-2930

Louisiana

Jefferson Parish Economic Development Commission
The Bid Center
1221 Elmwood Park Blvd., Suite 405
Harahan LA 70123
(504) 736-6550

Louisiana Productivity Center/USL
Procurement Technical Assistance Network
241 East Lewis St.
P.O. Box 44172
Lafayette LA 70504-4172
(318) 231-6422

NW Louisiana Government Procurement Center
Greater Shreveport Economic Development
400 Edwards St.
P.O. Box 20074
Shreveport LA 71120-0074
(318) 677-2530

Maine

Eastern Maine Development District
Market Development Center
One Cumberland Place, Suite 300
Bangor ME 04401
(207) 942-6389

Maryland

Morgan State University
School of Business Management
Cold Spring Lane & Hillen Road
Baltimore MD 21239
(410) 319-3861

Tri-County Council for Western Maryland
111 South George St.
Cumberland MD 21502
(301) 777-2158

Michigan

CEO Council, Inc.
Government Contracting Office
100 West Michigan, Suite 294
Kalamazoo MI 49007
(616) 342-0000

Downriver Community Conference
Local Procurement Office
15100 Northline
Southgate MI 48195
(313) 281-0700

Genesee County Metropolitan Planning Commission
Procurement Technical Assistance Center
1101 Beach St., Room 223
Flint MI 48502
(313) 257-3010

Jackson Alliance for Business Development
Center for State and Federal Procurement
133 West Michigan Ave.
Jackson MI 48201
(517) 788-4455

Northeast Michigan Consortium
320 State St.
Onaway MI 49765
(517) 733-8548

NW Michigan Council of Governments
Procurement Technical Assistance Center
P.O. Box 506
Traverse City MI 49685-0506
(616) 929-5036

Saginaw Future Inc.
Contact Procurement Office
301 East Genessee Ave., 3rd Floor
Saginaw MI 48607
(517) 754-8222

Schoolcraft College
Procurement Technical Assistance
18600 Haggerty Road
Livonia MI 48152-2696
(313) 462-4438

Thumb Area Consortium Growth Alliance
Local Procurement Office
3270 Wilson St.
Marlette MI 48453
(517) 635-3561

Warren Center Line
Sterling Heights Chamber of Commerce
30500 Van Dyke, Suite 118
Warren MI 48093
(313) 751-3939

West Central Michigan Employment and Training
Procurement Technical Assistance Center
110 Elm St.
Big Rapids MI 49307
(616) 796-4891

Minnesota

Minnesota Project Innovation
Procurement Assistance Center
111 Third Ave. South
Minneapolis MN 55401-2554
(612) 338-3280

Mississippi

Mississippi Contract Procurement Center
3015 12th St.
P.O. Box 610
Gulfport MS 39502
(601) 864-2961

Missouri

Curators of University of Missouri
University Extension
215 University Hall
Columbia MO 65211
(314) 882-0344

Montana

High Plains Development Authority
P.O. Box 2568
Great Falls MT 59403
(406) 454-1934

Montana TradePort Authority
115 North Broadway, Suite 200
Billings MT 59101-2043
(406) 256-6871

Procurement Technical Institute
305 West Mercury, Suite 208
Butte MT 59701-1659
(406) 723-4061

Nebraska

Nebraska Dept. of Economic Development
Existing Business Assistance Div.
301 Centennial Mall South, 4th Floor
Lincoln NE 68509-4666
(402) 471-3769

Nevada

State of Nevada
Commission on Economic Development
Capitol Complex
Carson City NV 89710
(702) 687-4325

New Hampshire

State of New Hampshire
Office of Business and Industrial Development
P.O. Box 856
Concord NH 03302-0856
(603) 271-2591

New Jersey

Elizabeth Development Corp.
Procurement Assistance Center
1045 East Jersey St.
P.O. Box 512
Elizabeth NJ 07207-0512
(908) 289-0262

New Jersey Institute of Technology
Defense Procurement Technical Assistance Center
240 Martin Luther King Jr. Blvd.
Newark NJ 07102
(201) 596-3105

New Mexico

State of New Mexico
Government Services Division
Procurement Assistance Program
1100 St. Francis Drive
Santa Fe NM 87503
(505) 827-0425

New York

Cattaraugus County
Dept. of Economic Development,
Planning and Tourism
303 Court St.
Little Valley NY 14755
(716) 938-9111

NY City Dept. of Businesses Services
Procurement Outreach Program
110 William St.
New York NY 10038
(212) 513-6472

NY State Dept. of Economic Development
Division of Small Business
One Commerce Plaza
Albany NY 12245
(518) 474-775

Rockland Economic Development Corp.
Procurement Technical Assistance Center
One Blue Hill Plaza, Suite 812
Pearl River NY 10965
(914) 735-7040

South Bronx Overall Economic Development Corp.
Economic Development Group
307 East 149th St.
Bronx NY 10455
(718) 292-3113

North Carolina

University of North Carolina
Small Business & Technology Development Center
4509 Creedmore Road
Raleigh NC 27612
(919) 571-4154

North Dakota

University of North Dakota
ND Small Business Development Center
P.O. Box 8164
Grand Forks ND 58202-8164
(701) 777-3700

Ohio

Central State University
Procurement and Technical Assistance Center
100 Jenkins Hall
Wilberforce OH 45384
(513) 376-6660

Columbus Area Chamber of Commerce
Central Ohio Government
Marketing Assistance Program
37 North High St.
Columbus OH 43215
(614) 225-6927

Community Improvement Corp. of Lake County
NE Ohio Government Contract Assistance Center
7750 Clocktower Drive
Mentor OH 44060-7595
(216) 951-8488

Greater Cleveland Growth Association
Cleveland Area Development Corp.
200 Tower City Center
50 Public Square
Cleveland OH 44113-2291
(216) 621-3300

Lawrence Economic Development Corp.
Procurement Outreach Center
101 Sand & Solida Roads
P.O. Box 488
South Point OH 45680
(614) 894-3838

Mahoning Valley Economic Development Corporation
Technical Procurement Center
4319 Belmont Ave.
Youngstown OH 44505-1005
(216) 759-3668

Terra Technical College
N. Central Ohio Procurement Technical Assistance Program
1220 Cedar St.
Fremont OH 43420
(419) 332-1002

University of Cincinnati
CECE-Small Business Development Center
111 Edison Drive
Cincinnati OH 45216-2265
(513) 948-2083

Oklahoma

Dept. of Vocational Technical Education
AVTS/Business & Industry Services
1500 West 7th Ave.
Stillwater OK 74074
(405) 743-5574

Tribal Government Institute
111 North Peters, Suite 204
Norman OK 73069
(405) 329-5542

Oregon

State of Oregon
Economic Development Dept.
775 Summer St. NE
Salem OR 97310
(503) 888-2595

Pennsylvania

Economic Development Council of Northeastern Pennsylvania
Procurement Technical Assistance Program
1151 Oak St.
Pittston PA 18640
(717) 655-5581

Geneva College
Government Procurement Assistance Center
3231 4th Ave.
Beaver Falls, PA 15010
(412) 847-4022

Indiana University of Pennsylvania
Government Contracting Assistance Center
Robertshaw Bldg., Room 10
650 South 13th St.
Indiana PA 15705-1087
(412) 357-7824

Johnstown Area Regional Industries Defense Procurement Assistance Center
111 Market St.
Johnstown PA 15901
(814) 539-4951

California University of Pennsylvania
Mon-Valley Renaissance
Government Agency Coordination Office (GACO)
California PA 15419
(412) 938-5881

NW Pennsylvania Regional Planning and Development Commission
Procurement Technical Assistance Center
614 Eleventh St.
Franklin PA 16323
(814) 437-3024

North Central Pennsylvania Regional Planning and Development Commission
Procurement Technical Assistance Center
651 Montmorenci Ave.
P.O. Box 488
Ridgway PA 15853
(814) 773-3162

Northern Tier Regional Planning and Development Commission
507 Main St.
Towanda PA 18848
(717) 265-9103

Private Industry Council of Westmoreland/Fayette, Inc.
Procurement Assistance Center
531 South Main St.
Greensburg PA 15601
(412) 836-2600

SEDA-Council of Governments
Procurement Technical Assistance Center
R.D. 1, Timberhaven
Lewisburg PA 17837
(717) 524-4491

Southern Alleghenies Planning and Development Commission
Government Procurement Program
541-58th St.
Altoona PA 16002-1193
(814) 949-6528

University of Pennsylvania
PASBDC-Snider Entrepreneurial Center
Philadelphia PA 19104-6374
(215) 898-1282

West Chester University
Center for the Study of Connectivity and Databases
128 Elsie O. Bull Center
West Chester PA 19383
(215) 436-3337

Puerto Rico

Commonwealth of Puerto Rico
Economic Development Administration
355 Roosevelt Ave.
Hato Rey PR 00918
(809) 753-6861

Rhode Island

**Rhode Island Port Authority
and Economic Development**
Financial Services
7 Jackson Walkway
Providence RI 02903
(401) 277-2601

South Carolina

University of South Carolina
Small Business Development Center
University of South Carolina
Columbia SC 29208
(803) 777-4907

South Dakota

**South Dakota Procurement Technical
Assistance Center**
School of Business
414 East Clark
Vermillion SD 57069
(605) 677-5287

Tennessee

University of Tennessee
Center for Industrial Services
226 Capitol Boulevard Bldg., S-606
Nashville TN 37219-1804
(615) 242-2456

Texas

Angelina College
Procurement Assistance Center
P.O. Box 1768
Lufkin TX 75902
(409) 639-1301

City of San Antonio
Procurement Outreach Program
P. O. Box 839966
San Antonio TX 78283
(512) 254-7135

El Paso Community College
P. O. Box 20500
El Paso TX 79998
(915) 594-2283

Northeast Texas Community College
East Texas Procurement Technical Assistance Program
P. O. Box 1307
Mt. Pleasant TX 75455
(903) 572-1911

Panhandle Regional Planning Commission
Economic Development Unit
P.O. Box 9257
Amarillo TX 79105-9257
(806) 372-3381

University of Houston/TIPS
Small Business Development Center
601 Jefferson, Suite 2330
Houston TX 77002
(713) 752-8477

University of Texas at Arlington
Automation and Robotics Research Center
Box 19125
Arlington TX 76019
(817) 794-5965

Utah

**Utah Department of Community
and Economic Development**
Utah Procurement Outreach Program
324 South State St., Suite 504
Salt Lake City UT 84111
(801) 538-8794

Vermont

State of Vermont
Agency of Development and Community Affairs
109 State St.
Montpelier VT 05609
(802) 828-3221

Virginia

Crater Planning District Commission
Procurement Technical Assistance Center
1964 Wakefield St.
Petersburg VA 23805
(804) 861-1667

George Mason University
Entrepreneurship Center
7960 Donegan Drive
Sudley North Building B
Manassas VA 22110
(703) 330-5091

Southwest Virginia Community College
Procurement Technical Assistance Center
P.O. Box SVCC
Richland VA 24641
(703) 964-2555

Washington

**Economic Development Council
of Kitsap County**
4841 Auto Center Way, Suite 204
Bremerton WA 98312
(206) 377-9499

**Economic Development Council
of Snohomish County**
917 134th St. SW, Suite 103
Everett WA 98204
(206) 743-4567

**Peninsula Technical Assistance
and Information Network**
P.O. Box 1012
Olalla WA 98359
(206) 857-3469

Spokane Area Economic Development Council
Local Business Assistance
N. 221 Wall, Suite 310
Spokane WA 99210-0203
(509) 624-9285

West Virginia

Mid-Ohio Valley Regional Council
Procurement Technical Assistance Center
P.O. Box 247
Parkersburg WV 26102
(304) 295-8714

Regional Contracting Assistance Center
1116 Smith St., Suite 202
Charleston WV 25301
(304) 344-2546

Wisconsin

Madison Area Technical College
Small Business Procurement Technical Assistance
211 North Carroll St.
Madison WI 53703
(608) 258-2330

Wisconsin Procurement Institute
840 Lake Ave.
Racine WI 53403
(414) 632-6321

Federal Information Centers

Call the number below that serves your area for answers to questions about the federal government. Each number serves the entire state or a major metropolitan area. If there is more than one number for your state, call the one for the city closest to you. For more information about Federal Information Centers, see page 29.

Alabama : (800) 366-2998

Alaska : (800) 729-8003

Arizona: (800) 359-3997

Arkansas: (800) 366-2998

California: (800) 726-4995
(Los Angeles, San Diego, San Francisco, Santa Ana)

California: (800) 726-4995
(Sacramento)

Connecticut: (800) 347-1997

Florida: (800) 347-1997

Georgia: (800) 347-1997

Hawaii : (800) 733-5996

Illinois: (800) 366-2998

Colorado : (800) 359-3997

Indiana : (800) 366-2998
(Gary)

Indiana: (800) 347-1997
(Indianapolis)

Iowa: (800) 735-8004

Kansas: (800) 735-8004

Kentucky: (800) 347-1997

Louisiana: (800) 366-2998

Maryland : (800) 347-1997

Massachusetts: (800) 347-1997

Michigan: (800) 347-1997

Minnesota: (800) 366-2998

Missouri: (800) 366-2998
(St. Louis)

Missouri: (800) 735-8004
(All locations other than St. Louis)

Nebraska: (800) 366-2998
(Omaha only)

Nebraska: (800) 735-8004
(All locations other than Omaha)

New Jersey: (800) 347-1997

New Mexico: (800) 359-3997

New York: (800) 347-1997

North Carolina: (800) 347-1997

Ohio: (800) 347-1997

Oklahoma: (800) 366-2998

Oregon: (800) 726-4995

Pennsylvania: (800) 347-1997

Rhode Island: (800) 347-1997

Tennessee: (800) 347-1997
(Chattanooga)

Tennessee: (800) 366-2998
(Memphis, Nashville)

Texas: (800) 366-2998

Utah: (800) 359-3997

Virginia: (800) 347-1997

Washington: (800) 726-4995

Wisconsin: (800) 366-2998

TDD calls: (800) 326-2996
If your area is not listed, call (301) 722-9098

U. S. Government Bookstores

You can purchase any government publication from stores in your regional area or from the national office in Washington D.C.. References to useful government publications are sprinkled throughout this guide, but for an overview of the federal government's publication lists and services, see page 29.

Alabama

U.S. Government Bookstore
O'Neill Building
2021 Third Ave. N
Birmingham AL 35203
(205) 731-1056

California

U.S. Government Bookstore
ARCO Plaza, C-Level
505 S. Flower St.
Los Angeles, CA 90071
(213) 239-9844

U.S. Government Bookstore
Room 194, Federal Building
450 Golden Gate Ave.
San Francisco CA 94102
(415) 252-5334

Colorado

U.S. Government Bookstore
Room 117, Federal Building
1961 Stout St.
Denver CO 80294
(303) 844-3964

U.S. Government Bookstore
NW Banks Building
201 West Eighth St.
Pueblo CO 81003
(719) 544-3142

Florida

U.S. Government Bookstore
100 West Bay St., Suite 100
Jacksonville FL 32202
(904) 353-0569

Georgia

U.S. Government Bookstore
First Union Plaza
999 Peachtree St. NE, Suite 120
Atlanta GA 30309-3964
(404) 347-1900

Illinois

U.S. Government Bookstore
One Congress Center
401 South State St., Suite 124
Chicago IL 60605
(312) 353-5133

Maryland

U.S. Government Bookstore
Warehouse Sales Outlet
8660 Cherry Lane
Laurel MD 20707
(301) 953-7974

Massachusetts

U.S. Government Bookstore
Thomas P. O'Neil Bldg., Room 169
Boston MA 02222
(617) 720-4180

Michigan

U.S. Government Bookstore
Suite 160, Federal Building
477 Michigan Ave.
Detroit MI 48226
(313) 226-7816

Missouri

U.S. Government Bookstore
120 Bannister Mall
5600 E. Bannister Road.
Kansas City MO 64137
(816) 767-8233

New York

U.S. Government Bookstore
Room 110, Federal Building
26 Federal Plaza
New York NY 10278
(212) 264-3825

Ohio

U.S. Government Bookstore
Room 1653, Federal Building
1240 E. 9th St.
Cleveland OH 44199
(216) 522-4922

U.S. Government Bookstore
Room 207, Federal Building
200 N. High St.
Columbus OH 43215
(614) 469-6956

Oregon

U.S. Government Bookstore
1305 SW First Ave.
Portland OR 97201-5801
(503) 221-6217

Pennsylvania

U.S. Government Bookstore
Robert Morris Building
100 N. 17th St.
Philadelphia PA 19103
(215) 597-0677

U.S. Government Bookstore
Room 118, Federal Building
1000 Liberty Ave.
Pittsburgh PA 15222
(412) 644-2721

Texas

U.S. Government Bookstore
Room 1C50, Federal Building
1100 Commerce St.
Dallas TX 75242
(214) 767-0076

U.S. Government Bookstore
Texas Crude Building
801 Travis St., Suite 120
Houston TX 77002
(713) 228-1187

Washington

U.S. Government Bookstore
Room 194, Federal Building
915 Second Ave.
Seattle WA 98174
(206) 553-4270

Wisconsin

U.S. Government Bookstore
Reuss Federal Plaza, Suite 150
310 W. Wisconsin Ave.
Milwaukee WI 53203
(414) 297-1304

Washington DC

U.S. Government Printing Office
710 N. Capitol St. NW
Washington DC 20401
(202) 512-0132

U.S. Government Bookstore
1510 H St. NW
Washington DC 20005
(202) 653-5075

State Women's Business Advocates

There are currently advocates in about 40 states. Check the state-by-state listing below to see if there is one in your state. The advocates change frequently, so if you have trouble tracking down the one for your state, contact the Ohio office listed below. As the national association's clearinghouse, this office has the most current information about who is serving as an advocate. For more general information about this advocacy network, see page 32.

Alabama

Jack Crittenden
Alabama Center for Commerce
401 Adams Ave.
Montgomery AL 36130
(205) 242-0400

Alaska

Bill Paulick
Small Business Advocate
Division of Economic Development
Box 110804
Juneau AK 99811
(907) 465-2017

Arkansas

Berthenia Gill
Minority Business Development
Arkansas Industrial Development Comm.
1 State Capitol Mall, Room 4C300
Little Rock AR 72201
(501) 682-1060

Arizona

Hariett Barnes
Governor's Office of Women's Services
1700 West Washington, #420
Phoenix AZ 85007
(602) 542-1755

California

Charmaine Sonnier
Office of Small and Minority Business
Dept. of General Services
1808 14th St., Suite 100
Sacramento CA 95814
(916) 322-5060

Rieva Lesonsky
Editor-in-Chief
Entrepreneurial Group
2392 Morse Ave.
Irvine CA 92714
(714) 261-2325

Christina Backlund
California Dept. of Commerce
801 K St., Suite 1700
Sacramento CA 95814
(916) 445-6408

Colorado

Charlotte Redden
Women's Business Program
Office of Business Development
1625 Broadway, Suite 1710
Denver CO 80202
(303) 892-3840

Connecticut

Pat Koch
Executive Director, Small Business Division
Dept. of Economic Development
865 Brook St.
Rocky Hill CT 06067
(203) 258-4360

Delaware

Gary Smith
Small Business Advocate
Delaware Development Office
99 King's Hwy., Box 1401
Dover DE 19903
(302) 739-4271

Florida

Ms. Laurice Thompson
Advocate, Small and Minority Business
Florida Dept. of Commerce
102 W. Gaines St., 501C Collins Bldg.
Tallahassee FL 32399-2000
(904) 487-4698

Kate H. Hoelscher
Florida SBDC Network
University of West Florida
Bldg. 76, Room 231
Pensacola FL 32514
(904) 474-3016

Georgia

Hooper Wesley
Small and Minority Business Program
200 Piedmont Ave., Suite 1302
Atlanta GA 30334
(404) 656-6315

Jennifer Horton
Special Programs: SBDC
University of Georgia
111 E. Broad St., Chicopee Bldg.
Athens GA 30602
(404) 542-5760

Hawaii

Sandra Cirie
Business Advocate
Economic Development and Tourism
P.O. Box 2359
Honolulu HI 96804
(808) 586-2594

Idaho

Tammy Dickenson
Adm. Division of Community Development
State Department of Commerce
700 W. State St.
Boise ID 83720
(208) 334-2470

Illinois

Nancy Smith
Regional Manager
Women's Business Program
300 S. Riverside, Room 1975S
Chicago IL 60606
(312) 353-5000

Mollie Cole
Women's Business Advocate
Dept. of Commerce and Community Affairs
100 West Randolph, Suite 3-400
Chicago IL 60601
(312) 814-7176

Indiana

Ann Neal-Winston
Small Business Development Corp.
Women and Minorities in Business
1 North Capitol St., Suite 1275
Indianapolis IN 46204
(317) 264-2820

Steve Thrash
Executive Director
Indiana SBDCs
1 North Capitol St., Suite 420
Indianapolis IN 46204
(317) 264-2820

Iowa

Toni Hawley
New Business Development Manager
Dept. of Economic Development
200 East Grand Ave.
Des Moines IA 50309
(515) 242-4749

Kentucky

Ann Ross
Cabinet for Economic Development
Capitol Plaza Tower, 23rd Floor
Frankfort KY 40601
(502) 564-7140

Louisiana

Patricia Robinson
Department of Economic Development
State of Louisiana
P.O. Box 94185
Baton Rouge LA 70804-9185
(504) 342-5882

Maine

Joan Anderson-Cook
Deputy Commissioner
Office of Business Development
Dept. of Economic and Commercial Development
State House, Station 59
Augusta ME 04330
(207) 289-2656

Maryland

Janis Carmichael
Executive Director
Suburban Washington SBDC
9201 Basil Court, Suite 403
Landover MD 20785
(301) 925-5032

Massachusetts

Lynn Wachtel
Office of Minority and Women's Business
100 Cambridge St., 13th Floor
Boston MA 02202
(617) 727-8692

Michigan

Kathleen Mechem
Women's Business Ownership Advocate
Department of Commerce
P.O. Box 30025
Lansing MI 48909-7504
(517) 335-1835

Minnesota

Tracy Thompson
Director, Small Business Development Center
Winona State University
P.O. Box 5838
Winona MN 55987
(507) 457-5088

Mississippi

Motice Bruce
Associate Manager. Sr. Enterprise Development
Mississippi Dept. of Economic and
Community Development
P.O. Box 849
Jackson MS 39205
(601) 359-3448

Missouri

Sue McDaniel
Women's Council
Economic Development and Training
P.O. Box 1684
Jefferson City MO 65102
(314) 751-0810

Mary Dalton Selby
President, Women's Yellow Pages of St. Louis
107 Habecking Drive
St. Louis MO 63137
(314) 869-3315

Montana

Misty Hammerbacker
Disadvantaged Business Center
Dept. of Transportation, Hwy. Building
2701 Prospect Ave.
Helena MT 59620
(406) 444-6337

Barbara Berk
Minority Women's Economic Development Group
127 N. Higgins Ave.
Missoula MT 59802
(406) 543-3550

Nebraska

Evan McKinney
Small Business Division
Nebraska Dept. of Economic Development
301 Centennial Mall S., Box 94666
Lincoln NE 68509-4666
(406) 444-3494

Nevada

Helen Myers
Director, Office of Small Business
Nevada Commission on Economic Development
3770 Howard Hughes Parkway, #295
Las Vegas NV 89109
(702) 486-7282

New Hampshire

Michelle Sweet
Small Business Development Center
108 McConnell Hall
University of New Hampshire
Durham NH 03824
(603) 862-0710

New Jersey

Cindy Conrad
Senior Business Consultant
Small and Minority Business
Dept. of Commerce and Economic Development
Mary G. Roebling Bldg., CN-835
Trenton NJ 08625-0835
(609) 292-3862

Alyson B. Miller
Assistant State Director
New Jersey SBDC
180 University Ave.
Newark NJ 07102
(201) 648-5950

New Mexico

Ernestine Florez
Director, NM Commission on Status of Women
4001 Indian School NE
Santa Fe NM 87110
(505) 841-4662

Beverly J. Duran
Chairman, Carretas
1900 Seventh St., NW
Albuquerque NM 87102
(505) 764-0047

New York

Celia Gonzalez
C/O Assistant Director of Business Services
Women Minorities and Women in Business
#1 Commerce Plaza
Albany NY 12245
(518) 486-6688

Jeri Sedler
Editor At Large
Working Woman Magazine
230 Parks Ave.
New York NY 10169
(212) 555-9496

North Carolina

Henry Payne
Supervisor, Minority Women's Business
Enterprise Program
North Carolina Department of Administration
116 W. Jones St.
Raleigh NC 27603-8002
(919) 733-8965

Andrea Harris
N. Carolina Institute of Minority
Economic Development
P.O. Box 1307
Durham NC 27702
(919) 682-1940

Kathryn McKee
Center for Community Self Help
413 East Chapel Hill St.
Durham NC 27701
(919) 683-9686

North Dakota

Pat Graff
Director, Women's Business Development
1833 East Bismark Expressway
Bismarck ND 58501
(701) 221-5300

Ohio

Melody K. Borchers
Women's Business Resource Program
Ohio Dept. of Development
77 S. High St., 28th Floor
Columbus OH 43215
(800) 848-1300
(614) 466-4945

Oklahoma

Marketia Head
Women's Small Business Division
Department of Commerce
6601 Broadway Extension
Oklahoma City OK 73116
(405) 843-9770

Oregon

Clifford Freeman
Manager, Minority/Women and Emerging
Small Business
155 Cottage St. N.E.
Salem OR 97310
(503) 378-5651

Pennsylvania

Lenore Cameron
Director, Bureau of Women's Development
Department of Commerce
462 Forum Building
Harrisburg PA 17120
(717) 787-3339

Geri Swift
National Foundation of Women's Business Owners
Geri Swift Associates
8 Station Lane
Philadelphia PA 19118
(215) 248-7999

Grace McGartland
President, NAWBO
530 Hasting St.
Pittsburg PA 15206
(412) 661-8325

Rhode Island

Isaac Wallace
Coordinator, Minority Business Affairs
Dept. of Economic Development
7 Jackson Walkway
Providence RI 02903
(410) 277-2601

South Carolina

Adriene Wright
Small and Minority Business Assistance
1205 Pendleton St., Room 441
Columbia SC 29201
(803) 734-0657

South Dakota

Steve Withorn
Director, Minority Business Office
Governor's Office of Economic Development
711 Wells Ave., Capital Lake Plaza
Pierre SD 57501
(605) 773-5032

Don Greenfield
State Director, SBDCs
University of South Dakota
414 East Clark St.
Vermillion SD 57069
(605) 677-5272

Tennessee

Brenda Logan (DECD)
Women's Business Liaison
Department of Economic Development
Nashville TN 37243-0405
(800) 251-8594

Texas

Rose Batson
President, Women's Chamber of Commerce
505 E. Huntland, #270
Austin TX 78752-3714
(512) 346-2676

Barbara Wilson
Center for Women's Business Enterprise
301 Congress Ave., Suite 1000
Austin TX 78701
(512) 476-9700

Shawn Holt
Certification Coordinator
Small Business Division
Department of Commerce
P.O. Box 12728
Austin TX 78711
(512) 320-9549

Utah

Beth Quist
Chairperson
Governor's Commission for Women
2678 South Cave Hollow Way
Bountiful UT 84010
(801) 298-1659

Susan Yoshimura
Women's Business Ownership Rep.
Small Business Administration
2237 Wallace F. Bennett Federal Bldg.
Salt Lake City UT 84138
(801) 524-3203

Kathy Ricci
Director, U. of Utah SBDC Regional Center
102 West 500 South, Suite 315
Salt Lake City UT 84101
(801) 581-7905

Vermont

Curt Carter
Economic Development Department
109 State St.
Montpelier VT 05602
(802) 828-3221

Virginia

Esther H. Vassar
Director, Dept. Minority Small Business Enterprise
200-202 N. 9th St., 11th Floor
Richmond VA 23219
(804) 786-5560

Anabel Gray
4440 Rollingwood Ct.
Troutville VA 24175
(703) 977-1307

Cindy Arlington
Virginia SBDC
Department of Economic Development
P. O. Box 798
Richmond VA 23206-0798
(804) 371-8253

Washington

Kathy Norwood
Specialist, Ent. Minority Women's Business
2001 6th Ave., #2700
Seattle WA 98121
(206) 464-6282

James Medina
Director, Office of Minority and
Women's Business Enterprise
406 South Water
Olympia WA 98504-4611
(206) 753-9693

Washington DC

Wilma Goldstein
Executive Director
National Women's Business Council
Small Business Administration
409 Third St., SW, #7425
Washington DC 20416
(202) 205-3850

Charles Countee
Director, Office of Business and
Economic Development
717 14th St. NW
Washington DC 20036
(202) 727-6600

Margene Utley
Executive Director
Minority Business Opportunity Commission
2000 14th St. NW
Washington DC 20009
(202) 939-8780

Sharon Hadary
National Foundation for Women Business Owners
1377 K St. NW, Suite 637
Washington DC 20005
(301) 495-4975

Paula Breitweiser
National Association of Women Business Owners
1377 K St. NW, Suite 637
Washington DC 20005
(301) 608-2590

West Virginia

Elizabeth Older
Rural Business Development Specialist
Governor's Office of Community
and Industrial Development
1115 Virginia St. East
Charleston WV 25305
(304) 348-2960

Wisconsin

Mary Strickland
Women's Business Ventures
Department of Development
123 West Washington Ave.
P.O. Box 797
Madison WI 53707
(608) 266-0593

Wyoming

Paula Morton
Commission for Women
Hirschler Bldg., 2nd East
Cheyenne WY 82002
(307) 634-0659

National Association of Women's Yellow Pages

Check the state-by-state listing below to see if there is a Women's Yellow Pages publisher in your area. For more information about the Women's Yellow Pages, see page 37.

Alabama

Women's Yellow Pages of Greater Mobile
P.O. Box 6021
Mobile AL 36660
(205) 437-5320

Arizona

Greater Phoenix Women's Yellow Pages
4425 North Saddlebag Trail
Scottsdale AZ 85251
(602) 945-5000

California

Women's Yellow Pages and Referral Service
13601 Ventura Blvd., #221
Sherman Oaks CA 91423
(818) 995-6646

Enterprising Women
Central Coast Yellow Pages for Women
P.O. Box 221974
Carmel CA 93922
(408) 455-0564

Women's Yellow Pages of Santa Clara County
10225 Imperial Ave.
Cupertino CA 95014
(408) 937-1801

Colorado

Front Range Women, Inc.
1900 Wazee St., Suite 206
Denver CO 80202
(303) 296-3447

Florida

South Florida Women in Business
Mirage Enterprises
7261 SW 152 St.
Miami FL 33167
(305) 251-0724

Georgia

Women's Yellow Pages of Greater Atlanta
P.O. Box 687
Alpharetta GA 30239
(404) 772-0050

Illinois

Women in Business Yellow Pages
Metro Chicago and Springfield
7358 North Lincoln, Suite 150
Chicago IL 60646
(708) 679-7800

Indiana

Indiana Women's Yellow Pages
6481 Taft, 2nd. Floor
Merrillville IN 46410
(219) 985-1120

Kansas

Women's Yellow Pages Directory
Greater Kansas City & Missouri
10308 Metcalf Plaza Bldg., Suite 178
Overland Park KS 66212-1804
(913) 341-4940

Louisiana

The Louisiana Women's Yellow Pages
P.O. Box 4301
Lafayette LA 70502
(318) 233-8973

Maryland

Women's Yellow Pages of Maryland
2238 Bay Ridge Ave.
Annapolis MD 21403
(410) 267-0886

Massachusetts

Greater Boston Women's Yellow Pages
P.O. Box 795
North Scituate MA 02060
(617) 545-9141

Missouri

St. Louis Women's Yellow Pages
107 Habacking Dr.
St. Louis MO 63137
(314) 869-3315

Women's Yellow Pages Directory
Greater Kansas City & Missouri
10308 Metcalf Plaza Bldg., Suite 178
Overland Park KS 66212-1804
(913) 341-4940

Nevada

Women's Yellow Pages of Nevada
3021 Valley View, Suite 209
Las Vegas NV 89102
(702) 598-3171

New York

Ask-Women's Business Resource Guide for New York State
93 Fruehauf Ave.
Snyder NY 14226-3805
(716) 839-0855

Ohio

Women's Yellow Pages/Greater Cleveland
Whittaker Publications
P.O. Box 24341
Highland Heights OH 44124-0341
(216) 646-0776

Oklahoma

The Women's Yellow Pages
P.O. Box 54475
Oklahoma City OK 73154
(405) 524-7020

Pennsylvania

The Greater Philadelphia Women's Yellow Pages
P.O. Box 1002
Havertown PA 19083
(215) 446-4747

South Carolina

The Greater Columbia Women's Yellow Pages
728 Seton Road
Columbia SC 29212-3333
(803) 772-3608

Texas

Women's Yellow Pages of Greater Dallas
18782 Vista Del Sol
Dallas TX 75287
(214) 931-9146

Virginia

The Women's Yellow Pages of Greater Richmond
11800 Midlothian Turnpike, Suite 200
Midlothian VA 23113
(804) 379-9710

Washington

Women's Yellow Pages
1427 27th Ave.
Seattle WA 98122
(206) 726-9687

Wisconsin

Women's Yellow Pages/Greater Milwaukee
P.O. Box 13827
Milwaukee WI 53213
(414) 789-1346

Canada

Women in Business Network Directory
1800-4th St. SW, Suite 1502
Calgary, Alberta T2S 2S2
(403) 244-1123

A Quick Guide to Common Terms

As you use this resource guide and talk with representatives of the programs that interest you, you may begin to feel overwhelmed with abbreviations, acronyms, and jargon. Here's a quick reference list of some of the most common terms you're likely to encounter.

MBDA: Minority Business Development Agency (Sponsored by the U.S. Department of Commerce to provide training, technical assistance and procurement assistance to minority business owners.)

MBE: Minority business enterprise

OSDBU: Office of Small and Disadvantaged Business Utilization (An OSBDU office has been established in all major federal agencies and departments to help small businesses sell their goods and services to the federal government.)

NAWBO: National Association of Women Business Owners (An influential national membership organization open to all women business owners.)

OWBO: Office of Women's Business Ownership (OBWO, sponsored by the SBA, develops specific programs designed to meet the special needs of women business owners.)

Procurement: The procedure used by purchasing agents in the public and private sector to obtain the goods and services needed to run their organizations. Contracts are awarded to qualified businesses based on a competitive bidding process.

Small business: As defined by the federal government, this is a business which is not dominant in its field and is independently owned and operated. In general, any business with fewer than 500 employees is defined as small, although some other standards, such as annual gross revenues, can apply.

SBA: Small Business Administration (The only federal agency whose sole responsibility is to foster the country's small business development.)

SBDC: Small Business Development Center (SBA-sponsored site for training, technical assistance and business counseling.)

SCORE: Senior Corps of Retired Executives (A group of volunteers who provide free business counseling.)

WBE: Women's Business Enterprise (Defined as a business enterprise which is at least 51% owned, controlled and run by women or a woman.)

About the Authors

Barbara Littman and Michael Ray are a husband and wife team with backgrounds in small business, marketing, education, writing and design.

Barbara is the founder of Information Design Northwest, a communications consulting firm specializing in training design, employee and technical communications and marketing materials. She works with a wide range of businesses, public agencies and independent consultants.

Michael, a former print and broadcast journalist, produces technical and marketing publications for a software development company, and does freelance business writing.

Barbara and Michael were partners in an educational toy business they sold in 1989.

Index

7(j) program, 7
8(a) businesses, 7
8(a) certification, 7

A

Alden Electronics, 54
Alliance of Minority Women for Business and Political Development, 58
American Business Women's Association (ABWA), 58
American Entrepreneurs Association (AEA), 64
American Management Association (AMA), 64
American Society of Women Accountants (ASWA), 61
American Women in Enterprise (AWE), 58
American Women's Economic Development Corp. (AWED), 13, 58, 77-78
An Income of Her Own, 14
Association for Women in Computing (AWC), 61
Association of African-American Women Business Owners, 58
Association of Black Women Entrepreneurs (ABWE), 58
Associations, professional, 61
Automated Business Locator System (ABELS), 49

B

Barbara Brabec Productions, 39
Bi-CAP, Inc., 78
Blue books, state, 34
Books
    For women only, 39
    See also Publications
Bookstores, U.S. Government, 116
BPW Foundation, 59
Business associations
    General, 64
    Women's, 58
Business Information Centers (BICs), 6, 27

C

CareerTrack, 22
Carroll Publishing Co., 34
CBD Fax Service, 55
CBD OnLine, 55
CBD Search Services, 55
Certification for women's businesses, 4
Chipps, Genie, 43
Cleveland Women's Business Development Center, 79
Coalition of 100 Black Women, 77
Columbus Area Chamber of Commerce, 79
Commerce Business Daily, 50
Committee of 200, 58

D

Danco, Katy, 40
Demonstration sites, 3
Departments of transportation
    State lists, 102
Dialog Information Services, 55

E

Economically disadvantaged minority programs, 7
Entrepreneur magazine, 44
Entrepreneurial training centers, 3
Entrepreneurial Training, Women's Network for, 13
EXCEL
    Midwest Women Business Owners Development Team, 78
EXCEL training program, 17

F

Family businesses
    Center for Family Business, 20
    Family Business Program, 21
Federal Information Centers, 28, 115
Financial Women International (FWI), 61
First-stop state offices, 91
Fred Pryor Seminars, 22

G

Girls
    Entrepreneurial training, 14, 16
Godfrey, Joline, 14, 41
Golant, Susan, 42
Government Access and Information Network (GAIN), 29, 55

H

Heim, Pat, 42
Helgesen, Sally, 42
Home businesses
    Barbara Brabec Productions, 39
    Home Office Computing magazine, 44
    National Association for the Cottage Industry, 64

I

Impact Business Consultants, 9
INC. magazine, 44
Institute for Professional Business Women, 14
International Alliance, The (TIA), 59

J

Jessup, Claudia, 43
Jinnett, Jerry, 43

K

Key Productivity Center, 22
Kozmetsky, Ronya, 43

L

Larkin, Geraldine, 42
Leads Club, The, 65
Lester, Mary, 42

M

Mackoff, Barbara, 42
Magazines, 43
Maldan Management Company, Inc., 78
Marketing to Women newsletter, 36
MBDA, 8-9
MBDA regional offices, 87
Mead Data Central, 55

Mentorship program, 2
Mercury Electronic Publishing, 55
Mi Casa Business Center for Women, 77
Milano, Carol, 41
Minority Business Development Agencies
    Regional offices, 87
Minority Business Development Agency (MBDA), 8-9
Minority Business Development Centers (MBDCs), 8
Minority Enterprise Development (MED) Week, 9
Minority Small Business Office, 8
Minority-owned businesses, 8
Ms. magazine, 44

N

National Alliance of Business (NAB), 64
National Association for Female Executives (NAFE), 60
National Association for the Cottage Industry (NACI), 64
National Association for the Self Employed (NASE), 64
National Association for Women Business Owners (NAWBO), 59
National Association for Women in Careers, 59
National Association of Black Women Attorneys (NABWA), 61
National Association of Minority Women in Business (NAMWIB), 59
National Association of Private Enterprise (NAPE), 64
National Association of Women Business Owners, 79
National Association of Women in Construction (NAWIC), 62
National Association of Women in Insurance (NAWI), 61
National Association of Women Lawyers (NAWL), 62
National Association of Women's Business Advocates (NAWBA), 32
National Association of Women's Yellow Pages, 37
    State offices, 125
National Business Association (NBA), 65
National Business Incubation Association (NBIA), 21
National Businesswomen's Leadership Association, 15
National Chamber of Commerce for Women, 15, 60
National Education Center for Women in Business (NECWB), 16, 38
National Federation of Business and Professional Women's Clubs (BPW), 59
National Federation of Independent Business, 65
National Foundation for Women Business Owners (NFWBO), 17, 38, 59
National Minority Business Council (NMBC), 56, 65

National Women's Business Council (NWBC), 24
National Women's Economic Alliance Foundation (NWEAF), 59
NAWBO
    See National Association of Women Business Owners
New Jersey NAWBO EXCEL, 78

O

Office of Business Liaison, 28
Office of Procurement and Grants Management, 8
Office of Small and Disadvantaged Business Utilization (OSDBU), 47
    Specialists, 97
Office of Women's Business Ownership (OWBO), 2-4, 24, 46
    Demonstration sites, 77
    Representatives, 71
Ohio Women's Business Resource Network, 78
Online services, 49
    Procurement information, 54-55
    SBA Online, 26
    Women's Information Resource Exchange (WIRE), 36

OSDBU
    See Office of Small and Disadvantage Utilization
OWBO
    See Office of Women's Business Ownership

P

Pinson, Linda, 43
Printing office, U.S. Government, 29
Procurement, 47
    Certification program for women business owners, 49
    Office of, 8
    Publications, 47, 50
    Technical Assistance Centers, 52
Procurement Automated Source System (PASS), 46
Procurement Technical Assistance Centers, 52
    Listings, 107
Professional associations for women, 61
Publications
    Commerce Business Daily, 50
    Procurement, 46, 50
    Small Business Administration, 25
    U.S. Government, 34

R

Renaissance Business Associates (RBA), 65
Roddick, Anita, 40
Rossman, Marlene, 41

S

Sales Opportunity Services, 55
SBA
    See Small Business Administration

Index

SBDC
    See Small Business Development Centers
SBI program, 5
SCORE
    See Service Corps of Retired Executives
Selling to state governments, 52
Selling to the federal government, 46
Seminar providers, private, 22
Seminars, 15
Service Corps of Retired Executives (SCORE), 4
    Women's Business Ownership Coordinators, 4
    Women's Business Ownership Coordinators list, 85
Simmons Graduate School of Management, 18
Sinclair, Carole, 41
SkillPath Inc., 22
Small Business Administration, 7
    Answer Desk, 25
    Business Information Centers, 27
    Office of Procurement and Grants Management, 8
    Office of Women's Business Ownership (OWBO), 24, 46
    Procurement Automated Source System, 46
    Publications and videotapes, 25
    Regional offices, 69
    SBA Online computer database, 26
    SCORE Women's Business Ownership Coordinators, 85
    Seminars, 2
    Small Business Development Centers, 6
    Women's representatives, 71
Small Business Development Centers (SBDCs), 6
    Offices of state directors, 80
Small Business Institutes (SBI), 5
Society of Women Engineers (SWE), 62
Softshare Government Information Services, 54
Specialized training programs, OWBO, 2
State departments of transportation, 49, 102
State Executive Directory Annual, 33
State government resources, 12
State programs for women, 91
State women's business advocates, 118
Superintendent of Documents, U.S., 29

T

Taylor, Russel, 40

U

U.S. Department of Commerce
    Minority Business Development Agency (MBDA), 8, 49
    Office of Business Liaison(OBL), 28
U.S. Department of Labor
    Women's Bureau, 10
U.S. Government
    Bookstores, 116
    Printing Office, 29, 51
    Superintendent of Documents, 29

W

WBE
    See Women's Business Enterprise
WESST Corp., 78
White Earth Reservation Tribal Council, 78
Wider Opportunity for Women (WOW), 60
WNET Mentorship Program, 2
Women Entrepreneurs, Inc., 79
Women in Aerospace (WIA), 62
Women in Agribusiness (WIA), 62
Women in Communications (WIC), 62
Women in Franchising (WIF), 60
Women in Information Processing (WIP), 63
Women in Management (WIM), 63
Women Life Underwriters Confederation (WLUC), 63
Women's Bureau, U.S. Dept. of Labor, 10
    Regional offices, 89
Women's Business Advocates
    State lists, 118
Women's Business Development Center, Chicago, 4
Women's Business Development Centers, 3
Women's Business Development Corporation (Maine), 32
Women's Business Enterprise (WBE) certification, 49, 52
Women's Business Ownership certification, 4
Women's Business Resource Program, 33
Women's Commercial Funding, 19, 37
Women's Council of Realtors (WCR), 63
Women's Economic Assistance Ventures, 79
Women's Economic Round Table (WERT), 60
Women's Economic Self-Sufficiency Training Program, 77
Women's Economic Venture Enterprise, 77
Women's Education and Leadership Forum (WELF), 19
Women's Entrepreneurial Growth Organization, 79
Women's Information Bank (WIB), 20
Women's Information Resource Exchange (WIRE), 36
Women's Initiative for Self Employment, 77
Women's Network for Entrepreneurial Training (WNET), 2
Women's Work Force Network, 60
Women's Yellow Pages, 37
    State offices, 125
Working Woman magazine, 44
World Association of Entrepreneurs, 59

Y

Yellow Pages, Women's, 37

Z

Zuckerman, Laurie, 41

Women's Business Resource Guide

Submission and Correction Form

If you would like to have your organization considered for inclusion in the next edition (or have found errors in a listing) of *The Women's Business Resource Guide*, please fill out a copy of this form and send it along with any printed material you may have to:

Directory Editor
The Resource Group
P.O. Box 25505
Eugene OR 97402

Organization: _____

Contact: _____

Street Address or P.O. Box: _____

City, State, Zip: _____

Telephone: _____   FAX: _____

Please provide a brief description of your organization's activities (or describe the correction and the page number on which your entry appears):

Ordering Information

Single copies of this book are available for $21.95 postpaid. Allow 3-4 weeks for delivery (via 4th Class mail). Enclose an additional $2.00 for one-week delivery (via 1st Class mail).

Quantity	Title	Unit Price	Total
1	Women's Business Resource Guide	21.95	

$2.00 for faster shipping (if desired) _____

Total enclosed _____

VISA and MasterCard orders via telephone only: 1-800-858-9055

I would like a copy of the *The Women's Business Resource Guide*. Enclosed is my check or money order. Please mail the book to:

Name _____

Organization _____

Address _____

_____

Telephone _____

Send all orders to:
The Resource Group
c/o Information Design Northwest
P. O. Box 25505
Eugene OR 97402
(503) 683-5330

Unconditional Guarantee!
If you're not completely satisfied, return the book in good condition for a full refund.

Call (503) 683-5330 for discount information and shipping costs on larger orders. Purchase orders are welcome from SBDCs, schools, libraries and government agencies.